Egypt

Berlitz®

Egypt

Text by Lindsay Bennett
Editor: Media Content Marketing, Inc.
Photography: Pete Bennett
Cover photograph by Pete Bennett
Cartography by Raffaele Degennaro
Managing Editor: Tony Halliday

Ninth Edition 2002

Contacting the Editors

Every effort has been made to provide accurate information in this publication, but changes are inevitable. The publisher cannot be responsible for any resulting loss, inconvenience or injury. We would appreciate it if readers would call our attention to any errors or outdated information by contacting Berlitz Publishing, PO Box 7910, London SE1 1WE, England. Fax: (44) 20 7403 0290;
e-mail: berlitz@apaguide.demon.co.uk

Printed in Singapore by Insight Print Services (Pte) Ltd, 38 Joo Koon Road, Singapore 628990. Tel: (65) 6865-1600. Fax: (65) 6861-6438

060/209 RP

CONTENTS

- A ☛ in the text denotes a highly recommended sight

Egypt

EGYPT AND THE EGYPTIANS

Egypt's long and illustrious history seems to hold the modern world spellbound. The ancient Empire that flourished here from 2500 BC until just before the dawn of Christianity was, arguably, the greatest civilisation that the world has ever seen. Two hundred years ago, after Napoleon sent his army officers to explore the land and bring back the first hand-drawn impressions of half-buried statues and columns, the world couldn't get enough. When Howard Carter peered through the dusty air of Tutankhamun's tomb in 1922 and, in his own words, "wonderful things" met his eyes, he confirmed the immeasurable wealth of the Pharaohs, and when the backer of the dig, Lord Carnarvon, died suddenly only a few months later, *vox populi* blamed it on the curse of the Pharaohs mummy – and Hollywood was quick to feed our fantasies. Today, "pseudo-scientific" theories about the origin and purpose of the pyramids fill the stands of bookshops and the listings on documentary channels. Our interest and curiosity about Egypt is, it seems, insatiable.

Due to this unprecedented attention, people travel to Egypt with preconceived ideas, in addition to a sense of excitement and anticipation. But when it comes to the reality of the archaeological sites, nothing prepares you for their beauty, scale and magnificence. The colossal statues are overwhelming, the delicate grace of the tomb paintings breathtaking, the pyramids prodigious, and the huge temple complexes positively Herculean. One can see how archaeologists arrive for one season and never leave – the ruins and artefacts, like the enigmatic smile of the Sphinx, pose more questions than we have answers.

Livestock use the same method of transport as people for crossing the Nile.

There's no doubt that the mysteries of the ancient world are the lure that attracts the majority of visitors, yet there is much to be said of modern Egypt – the archaeological sites do not sit in a geographical or cultural vacuum. Twenty-first century Egypt is a land of contrasts, but some things never change. Just as in ancient times, without the River Nile, Egypt could not exist. The longest river in the world brings abundant water from the heart of Africa to irrigate a narrow verdant valley snaking its way through the hundreds of thousands of square kilometres of parched desert that constitute the modern state. Its flow is constant – never suffocated by the all-pervading sand or evaporated by the oppressive heat of the sun. All along its length, small villages of modest mud-brick houses sit surrounded by verdant crops. You'll see gaggles of geese and ducks waddling along the riverbanks, burdened donkeys treading steadfastly homeward, and oxen compliantly tilling the fields.

The people of Egypt give thanks to the Nile, but they worship Allah, and the haunting intonations of the *muezzin* drift across city and farmland calling the faithful to prayer. It is, however, the most liberal Muslim state in the Middle East with a constitution and judiciary based on Western democratic models, not *shariah* Muslim law. The country also has a small but well-integrated Christian community who worship the tenets of St. Mark. The Copts, as they are known, have brought forth many influential individuals, including Boutros Boutros Ghali, former Secretary General of the United Nations.

These interesting amalgams help to make Egypt such a fascinating destination to visit. So many seemingly contrary and opposing factors combine to make it unique. Over 90 percent of its land is uninhabited, contrasting with great centres of population, including the capital, Cairo, which is the largest city in Africa – a dusty, noisy, sprawling, neon-lit, crowded metropolis of more than 14 million people.

The majority of its population is urban-dwelling, yet it has family groups of Berber and Bedouin nomads who spend their entire lives in their barren desert homeland. Office workers function by the tick of the clock, watching the minutes pass, while farmers live by the season, marking time with the twice-yearly harvests.

Though most of its people claim descent from the ancient Egyptians, modern religious practices and social protocols are totally

Consumers inspect the produce at a bustling street market in Cairo.

divorced from those of their ancestors. In a country where tradition plays an overriding part of everyday life, one-third of its energy comes from the ultra-modern source of hydro-electricity.

It may be Egypt's position at the meeting point of three cultures – Africa, Europe and the Middle East – that accounts for its complexity. It has long been influenced by their differing traits, and has assimilated their various customs and practices. African gold brought wealth in ancient times, and the darker-skinned Nubians became invaluable trading partners to the ancient Egyptians; living around Aswan in the south, they remain close to their roots and their strong musical traditions.

When the Arabs took the country from the east they brought a new religion, art, and society that swept away much of what had come before. In the 18th and 19th centuries the Europeans arrived – one legacy of which is the English and French spoken by a good number of native Egyptians – and the *khedives* of

Sunset is a beautiful time of day nearly anywhere in Egypt, but most especially on the river Nile.

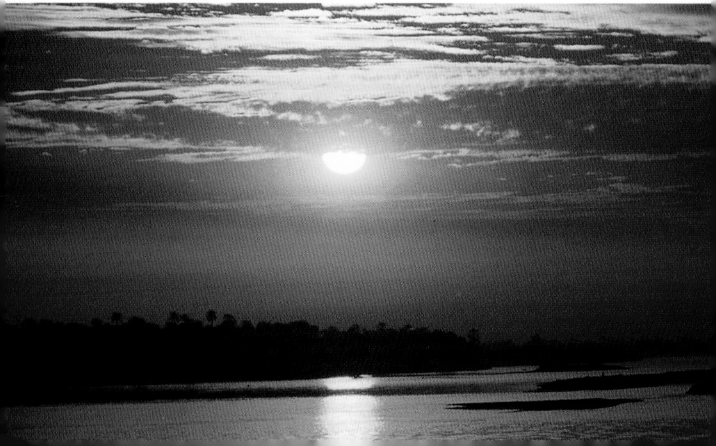

Egypt stole their ideas on administration and organisation to help them run the country.

Cairo, not Thebes, is the focus of today's Egypt. It was the pre-eminent city of the early Muslim era and the historic legacy of that time is a district of medieval Islamic architecture unrivalled anywhere in the world. The powerhouse of the modern economy, it is Cairo's role as a venue for peace talks, a focus for the Arab countries of the near east, and home of the Arab Council that is invaluable in these diplomatically uncertain times.

But tourism is the country's modern lifeblood, and not just as a result of our insatiable thirst for history. The seas that lap Egypt's arid shores hide pristine marine ecosystems that have lured scuba divers from the inception of the sport. Package tourists soon followed and today the coastline of Egypt is turning into a year-round playground. With daytime temperatures rarely dropping below the high 60s Farenheit (20°C) and almost continuous sunshine, it makes a welcome retreat from the drab northern European winters, and a scorching alternative to temperate summers. The authorities have been quick to respond, allowing hotels and other facilities to develop – though care must be taken not to blight the delicate environment in the rush to turn the resorts into "Euroland".

Not everything in the garden is rosy of course. With poverty and unemployment rising along with foreign debt, and Islamic fundamentalists spurning negotiation and resorting to violence, Hosny Mubarak, the nation's president since 1980, has enormous problems to solve. But with a foot in so many camps – past and present, East and West, religious and secular – Egypt should be well-placed to withstand the vagaries of modern life and grow in wealth and influence in the coming years. The kingdom of the Pharaohs has many more eras of history to add yet.

A BRIEF HISTORY

The fertile Nile Valley has supported human life for over 8,000 years. Stone Age settlers developed from hunters to farmers, growing barley and wheat crops that originated in Mesopotamia. Mesopotamian script was also copied, but it developed into the first Egyptian written language. From the earliest days Egyptians recorded their activities on papyrus, helping us to piece together the pivotal moments in the great days of the Ancient Egyptian Empire.

Ancient Egypt's complicated annals are filled with massive communal building projects and great individuals traced through many millennia. Archaeologists are still debating the exact chronology of certain Egyptian dynasties and individual rulers. However, general agreement exists on the division of history into set phases, giving a name to each. The Pre-Dynastic and Early Dynastic periods are followed by the Old, Middle, and New Kingdoms with Intermediate periods in between. These are followed by the Late, Macedonian and Ptolemaic periods until Egypt was absorbed into the Roman Empire in the 1st century AD.

The Pre-Dynastic and Early Dynastic Periods (5000–2780 BC)

For many years Egypt was not one kingdom but two – Upper Egypt in the south and Lower Egypt in the north. It was not until 3170 BC that King Narmer of Upper Egypt conquered Lower Egypt. Around 3100 BC the kingdoms of Upper and Lower Egypt were unified under King Menes – his crown was the first to depict the symbols of both kingdoms. He made his capital at Memphis in Lower Egypt (near present-day Cairo) and the first Dynasty was founded.

The Old and Middle Kingdoms

The Old Kingdom was established around 2780 BC and lasted more than five centuries. It heralded the first great phase of development in science and architecture; hieroglyphs were developed and the first great building phase took place.

Rulers began to grow more powerful and looked for some way to prove their might both in life and in death. King Djoser of the Fourth Dynasty was the first to attempt to build a large funerary monument to hold his mortal remains and protect the riches buried with him for his next life. The result is the step pyramid at Saqqara.

Other rulers followed suit and by 2526 BC the design had been perfected and the world was graced by the Great Pyramid at Giza built for Khufu (or Cheops). Not long before this time, between 2575–2550 BC, King Chephren had the Sphinx erected in his honour at Giza. It was at this momentous time that the first mummifications began. Khufu's son Redjedef made a monumental change to Egyptian life when he introduced the solar deity Ra, or Re, into the Egyptian religion. Worship of Ra would grow to become one of the most important facets of Egyptian culture over the next 3,000 years.

However, during the decisive years between 2140–2040 BC, a split occurred between the two Kingdoms when rival power bases arose in Heliopolis in Lower Egypt and Thebes (modern Luxor) in Upper Egypt. This is what archaeologists call the First Intermediate period. The Karnak temple at Thebes was begun around 2134 BC, marking the city's rise to prominence.

The Middle Kingdom, 2040–1801 BC, commenced with Theban rulers of the 11th Dynasty attempting to extend their control, and Egypt was reunified under Mentuhotep II. His

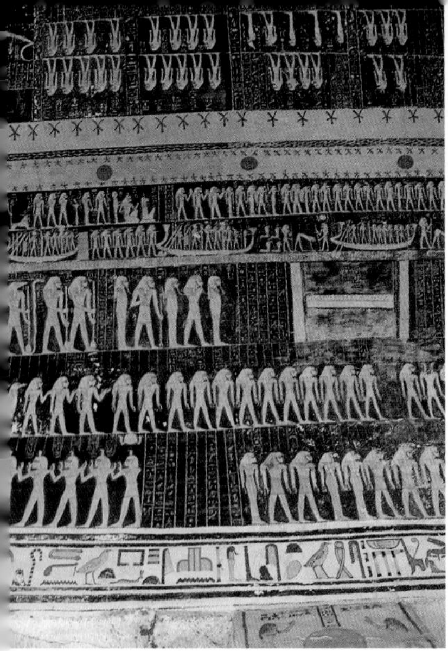

Detail of a tomb ceiling in the Valley of the Kings.

successors built a power base at Thebes, and started a cultural renaissance with wide-reaching effects on Egyptian art and archaeology.

The local Theban god Amon became intertwined with Ra creating the deity Amon Ra and around 1800 BC, the female Osiris cult developed into a main deity. Thebes held onto power until the 12th Dynasty, when its first king, Amenemhet I, who reigned between 1980–1951 BC established a capital near Memphis. However, he continued to give prominence to the Theban god Amon, ensuring that the worship spread across the kingdom.

But rival peoples coveted the riches of Egypt and sometime around 1600 BC, a people called the Hyskos invaded Lower Egypt from Libya, splitting the kingdom in two and starting the Second Intermediate period.

The New Kingdom (1540–1100 BC)

Hyskos rule lasted less than 100 years. They were driven out of Lower Egypt by Ahmose I who founded the 18th Dynasty, ruling over a united Egypt from the capital of Thebes. The pharaohs of the 18th Dynasty instigated many important reforms. They reorganised the army and consolidated power in the hands of family members at the expense of feudal leaders. Artistically and culturally Egypt reached its zenith during the New Kingdom and many of the most renowned pharaohs reigned during this time. The Valley of the Kings was also chosen as a new burial ground for the pharaohs when Tuthmoses I (1504–1492 BC) was entombed in a narrow valley across the river from the temple at Karnak.

Throughout the 1400s (BC) Karnak and Luxor temples were greatly expanded and several huge building projects took place on the west bank. However in 1356–1339 BC a new pharaoh, Amenophis IV, decided to leave Thebes and, with his wife Nefertiti, created a new capital on a virgin site at Tell El Amarna to the north. He introduced a monotheistic cult around the one true god – Aten – and changed his name to Akhenaten ("He who pleases Aten"). This sudden

In Thebes, the Valley of the Kings is now an immensely popular tourist destination.

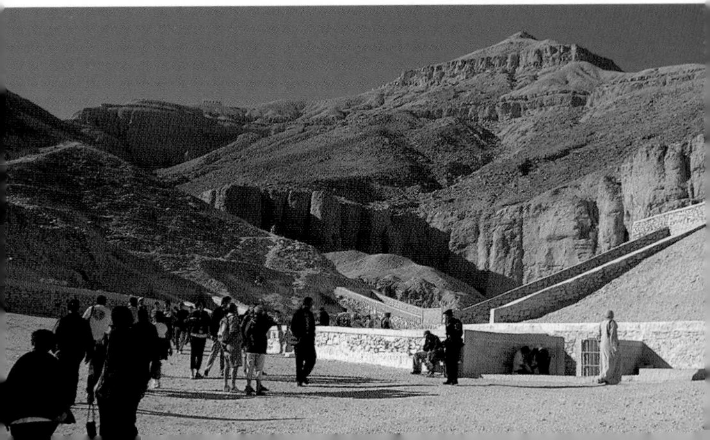

change brought chaos to Egypt and she lost international influence, but Akhenaten's successor – his son, the young Tutankhamun – brought power back to Thebes and reinvested the priests of Amon Ra and his fellow gods with religious supremacy.

Tutankhamun died in mysterious circumstances without an heir. His warrior successor, Ramses I, heralded the start of the 19th Dynasty, to be followed by Seti I (1291–1279 BC), who won back many of the lands lost during the Akhenaten years.

The 60-year rule of Ramses II (1279–1212 BC) was a great finale to the New Kingdom era. One of the most prolific

The Avenue of the Sphinxes is one of many important historical monuments at the Temple of Luxor.

builders in the history of Egypt ruled for over 60 years and supervised magnificent projects expanding Luxor and Karnak temples and creating the magnificent Abu Simbel. Some scholars now postulate that Ramses II was the Egyptian pharoah of Biblical fame who let the Jews leave his land for Israel.

Following Ramses II, Ramses III built a vast mortuary complex at Medinet Habu but power was already slipping from royal hands into those of the exclusive and secretive priesthood known as the servants of Amun-Ra. In 1070 BC the country was split again and foreign powers began to overrun the borders. By 715 BC Egypt was already dominated by foreign power – the Assyrians – and also began increasing trade and diplomacy with the expanding Roman Empire.

The Ptolemaic Period

In 332 BC Alexander the Great occupied Egypt and appointed Cleomenes of Naucratis, a Greek resident in Egypt and his Macedonian general, as governor. Then, after Alexander's death in 323 BC, Cleomenes took control of the country under the name Ptolemy I. The new city of Alexandria, located on the Mediterranean coast, became the base for the Ptolemaic control of Egypt and the cultural capital of Europe, and Thebes finally lost its influence. However, the Ptolemies were responsible for building and refurbishing several important temples in Upper Egypt, including Denderah, Philae and Edfu. They adopted Egyptian gods as their own and did much to prolong Egyptian culture rather than simply converting it to Greek.

The Ptolemaic era came to an end with its most famous ruler, Queen Cleopatra. During her lifetime (69–30 BC), the infamous queen attempted to link her land to Rome

Cleopatra appears in hieroglyph form at the Temple of Denderah.

through her liaison with Julius Caesar. Their son Caesarean would have ruled over both countries, thus continuing the Egyptian blood line. However, events turned profoundly against Cleopatra when Caesar was suddenly killed and she fled back to Alexandria to commit suicide in 30 BC. Egypt was reduced to a provincial status in the Empire – it was ruled first from Rome and subsequently from Constantinople.

The Arab Empire

Egypt was caught up in the first wave of Moslem Arab expansion in the 630s AD, less than ten years after the death of the prophet Mohammed. His teachings were encapsulated in the Koran and they fired the previously disparate Arab tribes to spread the word of Allah. Egypt became one of the most influential Arab states, especially when, in the mid-9th century, a more powerful Arab force – the Fatimids – swept across Egypt from the west. They established a capital called Al-Qahira – "the City of Victory" – known to the modern world as Cairo.

Over the next two centuries, Cairo became a centre of culture and learning that was unsurpassed in the Islamic world with the establishment of the renowned El-Azhar University and mosque. In 1169 the Fatimids were crushed by the armies of Saladin – already flush with victories in Palestine and Syria – who established the Ayyubid Dynasty and created the fortified citadel to protect Cairo. However Ayyubid control was weak and power was usurped by their Turkish slaves, called *mamelukes*, who succeeded in founding a dynasty that lasted from 1251 to 1517. In Cairo they built vast palaces and ornate mosques, and expanded the influence of the great Khan el-Khalili market to expand Egypt's trading power.

Mameluke power was taken by Ottoman Turks in 1517, but little changed on a day-to-day basis as the Turks preferred to use local people to control their more remote dominions. They appointed an overall governor, or Pasha, who then organised the country to his own liking with mameluke help. Egypt became a backwater – even more so as the Ottoman Empire went into chronic terminal decline in the 18th century, with a series of crises that local mamelukes were unable to control.

As Ottoman control weakened, Egypt became a pawn in a larger game. In 1798 a young Napoleon Bonaparte, eager to curtail growing British power, arrived in Egypt and after a short and decisive battle claimed, he the country for France. He set about forming a ruling body, and sent scholars and artists out into the countryside to explore and record its ancient treasures – thus sparking the great interest in Egyptology among scholars in France and the rest of Western Europe.

His stay was short-lived however; the British fleet were after him and inflicted a devastating defeat on the French

Navy at the battle of Aboukir later the same year. Napoleon went home to claim 'victory' but he had to leave the bulk of his army behind. Meanwhile an Ottoman force had been dispatched from Istanbul to counter the French. They were led by Mohammed Ali, a brilliant intellectual who, in the aftermath of the French withdrawal, asked to be appointed Pasha of Egypt. The Ottoman Sultan agreed to his request and he set about establishing his power base. In 1811 Mohammed organised a grand banquet and called all the notable mamelukes to attend. Once they were all at his compound he had them massacred – their influence had come to a sudden, bloody end.

Mohammed Ali had a vision for his new domain. He admired Western military tactics and set about modernising the army and navy. Agriculture and commerce were brought up-to-date and cotton was introduced as a commercial crop. Cairo saw a rash of new building that expanded the city's boundaries. The new ruler grew wealthy and powerful, twice declaring war on his sovereign and almost beating the sizeable but dissolute Ottoman army. Istanbul was forced to recognise this powerful thorn in its side as a semi-autonomous part of the Empire, and granted hereditary status to the role of Pasha of Egypt. Later the title was upgraded to *khedive*, the equivalent of Viceroy.

The House of Mohammed Ali, however, ultimately failed to live up to its founder's great achievements, as the ruling body increasingly grew to be corrupt and recklessly irresponsible. The one great feat that was achieved during their sovereignty, though, was the creation of the Suez Canal, an engineering marvel of its day that opened with great aplomb in 1869.

The Khedive Ismael had extravagant plans for numerous great works that were to be financed by Western European powers, but when he became stuck in a financial quagmire, they insisted on bringing in their own advisors to control key institutions. The British soon had an unassailable grip on Egyptian politics and commerce.

The 20th Century

As European power-brokering turned into World War I, Egypt became vital to the British, being close to the enemy Ottoman heartland, and allowing quick passage through the Suez Canal to her dominions in India, the Far East, Australia and New Zealand. When the Ottoman Empire crumbled in the aftermath of the war, Egypt declared itself an independent kingdom, but real power remained in London. A strong independence party, the Wafd, gained political power during the 1920s and became a prominent force throughout the next few decades.

The mosques of Sultan Hasan and Rifal stand prominently in this sweeping view of Cairo.

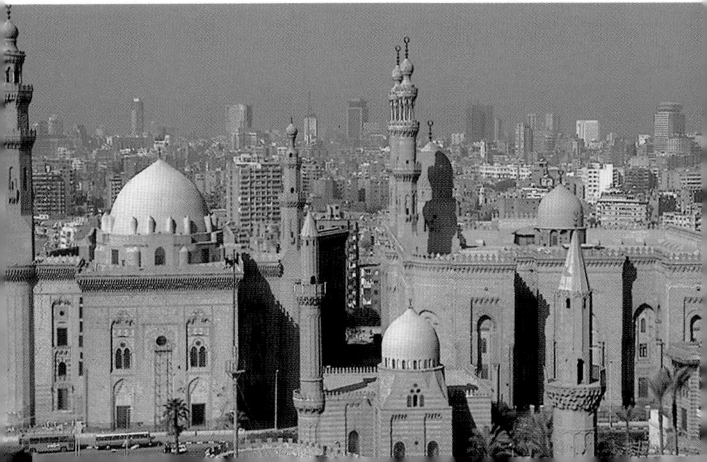

In World War II Hitler and Mussolini recognised that the Suez Canal was vital to British plans, and Egypt – along with the rest of North Africa – became an important field of battle. Axis forces were at one point only 241 km (150 miles) from Cairo but Allied soldiers finally gained the upper hand following the British victory at El Alemain in 1942, and Egypt remained firmly in British hands for the rest of the war.

Post-war politics brought a new set of problems. The new Jewish state of Israel founded on land so recently Islamic Palestine sent shockwaves through the Arab world and Egypt found itself at the centre of a bloody defeat in 1948 when it stood up against its new neighbour.

King Farouk, who had come to the throne in 1936, was seen as a playboy with a love of luxurious living. When he attempted to restore national pride by wresting the Suez Canal out of British hands he suffered an embarrassing diplomatic defeat and, at home, unrest turned to opposition.

In June 1952 a group of high-ranking military officers declared a military coup. Led by Colonel Gamal Abdel Nasser, they drove Farouk into exile and nationalised the Suez Canal. Nasser was to rule for 17 years, during which, with Soviet help, Egypt embarked on a huge modernisation programme. Chief

A WWII memorial stands in El Alamein at the Allied Cemetery.

among its projects was the Aswan High Dam, which provided hydroelectricity to the population and freed the country from the scourge of the annual river flood, bringing security to the highly populated Nile Delta.

Anwar el-Sadat succeeded Nasser in 1970. He was not as charismatic as Nasser and, though he had a more moderate stance, became embroiled in several unsuccessful short wars with Israel that severely weakened the country and left the Sinai region in Israeli hands. Limited success in 1973 restored some national pride when the Sinai was returned, but Sadat was aware that his country could be bled dry if the conflict continued. In 1979 Egypt became the first Arab state to recognise the state of Israel – other Arab states were aghast and internal opposition to Sadat grew. In 1981 he was assassinated by an army officer while at a military parade.

Since then Hosny Mubarak has been Egypt's president. He has worked hard to find a place for Egypt at the negotiation table, acting as a moderator and offering Cairo as a venue for Arab/Israeli peace talks throughout the 1980s and 90s. Mubarak's pragmatic approach has earned him many admirers, but also some enemies – not least among them, extremists within his own country. During the 1990s they made numerous attempts to de-stabilise his regime, finally resorting to attacking the mainstay of the Egyptian economy – tourism – and several despicable attacks on foreign visitors resulted in over 60 deaths. A number of trials are said to have put the instigators in prison and security measures have been enhanced, but their actions did a great deal of damage from which Egypt will be slow to recover. Tourism numbers fell dramatically but are now rising again as visitors grow more confident. Meanwhile, the vast majority of ordinary Egyptians, who offer a warm welcome to tourists, put their faith in Allah for an upturn in their economic fortunes.

WHERE TO GO

CAIRO AND THE PYRAMIDS

Founded in 641 and expanded by the Fatimids in the 9th century, Cairo – Al-Qahira or "the City of Victory" – became one of the most powerful Islamic cities in the world during the Medieval era, marking a rebirth in Egypt's fortunes. Situated where the Nile valley widens to become the Nile Delta, it is now the largest city in Africa with a population of over 14 million people. It's hot, dusty and noisy; its roads often at gridlock; its public transport system for the most part in chaos. However, once you accept these facts, Cairo has lots to offer the visitor; its main museum is an essential part of your holiday experience and its street life is a sure sign that you have come to a totally different culture.

Central Cairo

Central Cairo is based around the River Nile, and several modern streets and squares where you'll find most of the international hotels. **Tahrir Square** (Liberation Square) on the east bank is Cairo's heart, a mass of streets converging on the biggest bus terminus in the city, which is bounded by government ministries and office blocks housing airline offices and travel agencies. Nearby on the banks of the river is the **Nile Hilton Hotel** – a landmark for Cairenes (as the people of the city are known) as well as tourists. Leading east from the square is Kasr El-Nil Street lined with Western-style shops and restaurants. Nearby **Ramses Square** plays host to the Victorian Railway Station, designed in the heyday of colonialism and fronted by a monumental granite statue of Ramses II transported from the ancient Egyptian capital of Memphis in 1955.

Out in the river are several islands; the largest one, **Gezira**, is home to one of Cairo's most chic neighbourhoods, **Zamalek**. You'll find a number of things to do here. The **Gezira Sporting Club** has a range of facilities that you can enjoy as a temporary member, but if you don't feel energetic, you could try an evening of music – the contemporary **Opera House** is located here, sharing a complex with the **Modern Art Museum**. You can get an excellent view of the cityscape from the **Cairo Tower** (El-Borg), designed to imitate a minaret, though it does stand significantly higher at 182 metres (600 ft) above the city.

South of Gezira is **Roda Island**, home to **Manial Palace**, now converted into an art gallery. The **Nileometer** is also situated here. It was built in AD 715 to help measure the peak and trough of the Nile flood. It's now no longer needed as the Aswan High Dam in the far south of Egypt completely controls the flow, keeping the city safe.

The Cairo Tower stands tall on Gezira Island.

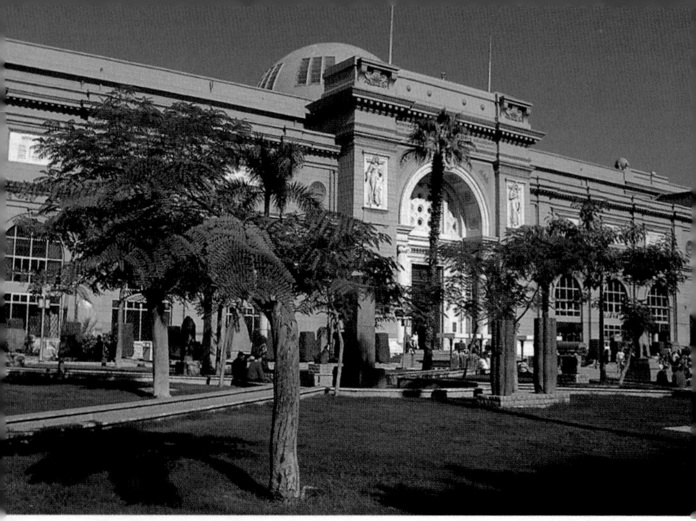

The gardens and entrance to the Egyptian Museum. You'll need to visit more than once to fully appreciate the collection.

The west bank of the Nile is home to the modern university and seemingly endless residential suburbs, but two attractions lie on or close to the river. In the north, opposite Gezira Island, the **Egyptian National Circus**, a Soviet-trained troupe, performs nightly except in summer. Further south, set among verdant gardens, is the **Cairo Zoo**.

The Egyptian Museum

Sitting on the north side of Tahrir Square is the **Egyptian Museum**, built in 1902 as the Cairo Museum. Founded by French architect Auguste Mariette in an attempt to stop the flow of artefacts to museums around the world, it has grown into one of the major collections in the world, housing some of the finest treasures of the ancient Egyptian civilisation.

The museum is a little dated, confusing, and often crowded – the best time to visit is at lunchtime when most large groups are having lunch – but with over 120,000 pieces on display, all between 5,000 and 1,400 years old, it is a must-see attraction during your visit. The artefacts in the museum come from archaeological sites around the country and they will add a great deal to your understanding and appreciation of ancient Egypt. Allow at least two hours for the visit – a comprehensive tour will take three or four. The best strategy is to schedule two visits into your itinerary, one each before and after your trips to the temples and other historical sites along the Nile.

The artefacts that most people put at the top of their lists are on the second floor, so you may want to head there first before you get worn out. Several recently refurbished rooms display over 1,700 objects found at the tomb of Tutankhamun by Howard Carter in 1922. The only undisturbed royal tomb ever to be found in the Valley of the Kings, it captured the public imagination and fired peoples' desire to visit Egypt. The king was only 19 when he died and there was little time to prepare a larger tomb, but it was still filled with treasures for use when Tutankhamun arrived in the Other World. In the years following his interment, the tomb entrance became covered with debris when another tomb was dug nearby, saving it from tomb robbers. Three coffins surrounding the king's mummy are on display at the museum – the inner one is fashioned from pure gold and weighs 170 kg (374 lbs). The king's gold funerary mask can also be seen, a truly awe-inspiring find which still dazzles the eye even after over 3,000 years.

Also upstairs is the Mummy Room where you can find the preserved remains of some of Egypt's most illustrious rulers. These mainly date from the 18th to the 20th dynasties and include Ramses IV, Seti I and Tutmosis III. Though Tutankhamun could have been among them, the Egyptian authorities made the decision to return him to the Valley of the Kings and he now rests once again in the inner sanctuary of his tomb in a stone sarcophagus.

The ground floor rooms follow the chronological history of ancient Egypt starting on the left of the entrance with the Old Kingdom Room. The finds are mainly tomb artefacts found at sites across the country and you can view the exact re-creation of a funerary chamber found at Dahshur to familiarise yourself with what you will see later in your holiday along the Nile Valley in Upper Egypt.

Security Measures

Several terrorist attacks in the 1990s caused the Egyptian authorities to put extra security measures in place to protect visitors. These are enforced at the Egyptian Museum but are more noticeable when you are touring the temples in Upper Egypt. All foreign travellers to Egypt must be accompanied by a military guard and to make this easier, a timed convoy system has been put into place. This means that tour buses, taxis and private hire cars must only travel with the convoy and must report at a certain time to travel. If you book a tour with a company they will make the arrangements and incorporate it into your tour timetable. If you travel by taxi make sure that your driver knows what time the convoy to a certain destination is leaving. If travelling independently, check in with the local police station and they will provide you with the details.

A moment of tranquillity in the interior courtyard of the el-Nasir mosque, inside the Citadel of Cairo.

Tomb artefacts give us a great deal of information about daily life in Egypt. There are delightful wooden figures made as servants for the dead; these included guards, and craftsmen and boat crews with their boats. Important foodstuffs like ducks and cattle were re-created in wood to make sure that the king would be provided for in his afterlife.

Room Three is devoted to the so-called heretic period of Egyptian history when Ahkenaten established a religion based on only one god and founded a capital at Tell al Amarna in central Egypt. The experiment lasted only until Ahkenaten's death when almost all records relating to him were destroyed. All the artefacts here were excavated at Tell al Amarna including two giant statues of Ahkenaten himself, with his distinctive long chin and rounded belly.

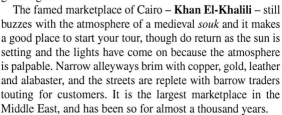

Among this amazing range of exquisite and colourful finds, there are also important artefacts that help confirm certain archaeological theories about the chronology of Egyptian history, such as the slate palate of King Narmer – one of the first documents scribed after Egypt became a unified kingdom.

Statuary found all around the kingdom depict both the important deities – Osiris, Hathor, Isis and others – and the pharaohs of the major dynasties. Huge representations of rulers like Ramses II illustrate the power held by the throne and by the cult of personality, though there are also tiny sculptures such as a bust of Queen Hatschepsut, which may have stood on a mantle or in a niche, showing that Egyptians were not just fixated by the epic and monumental.

Islamic Cairo

Though Cairo has many modern and nondescript suburbs, the oldest districts of Al-Qahira are well-preserved and exhibit some of the finest period architecture in the Islamic world. Founded to the east of the river, Cairo was protected from the yearly Nile flood and surrounded by a high wall to guard against invaders.

The famed marketplace of Cairo – **Khan El-Khalili** – still buzzes with the atmosphere of a medieval *souk* and it makes a good place to start your tour, though do return as the sun is setting and the lights have come on because the atmosphere is palpable. Narrow alleyways brim with copper, gold, leather and alabaster, and the streets are replete with barrow traders touting for customers. It is the largest marketplace in the Middle East, and has been so for almost a thousand years.

The market developed during the Fatimid period on the main street of Cairo, which connected the main city gates of Bab Zuweila in the south and Bab El-Futah in the north. A series of *caravanserais* (rooming houses for the camel caravans that were the main method of transporting goods), or *khans* as they were known in Egypt during the Fatimid era, were built here by Emir El-Khalili, giving the market its name. As you stroll along its various shopping streets, look for significant Islamic monuments. Exquisite stone carving, wood turning, copper/brasswork and ceramic tiling are the main features of Islamic architecture and the period buildings, mosques, *madrasas* (Islamic religious schools), *khans* and *bayts* (private homes) are very impressive.

Major among these is the **Kalawun** and **Barquq Mosque** on the arterial Muizz lidina-Illah Street. Dating from 1293, its long façade is rich in architectural detail. The tomb of Al-Mansur Kalawan (died 1290) is at the heart of the complex and is surrounded by beautiful screens of ornate Islamic fretwork.

If the striking portal of the El-Nasir Mohammed *madrasa* next door strikes you as reminiscent of those in European Gothic churches, you are not far from the truth. The stone was taken as booty from a Crusader church in Acre (now Israel) when it was overrun by Arab forces. The Barquq Mosque is the youngest in the complex, completed in the late 14th century.

Continue north and then left on A-Darb al-Asfar Street, and you'll find **Bayt es-Suheimi** on your right. This was the residence of the rector of the El-Ahzar Mosque until 200 years ago. Islamic homes centred around a large central hall called a *qa'a* with a fountain in the middle. The *qa'a* led to the family rooms. Light was supplied via a dome *(schukhsheikha)* in the roof as the windows were covered by ornate wooden covers. The former rector's house has been fully restored and offers an excellent example of fine Cairene architecture.

From here it's only a short walk to the **Mosque of al-Hakim** and **Bab El-Futah** set in a remaining section of the original city wall. The mosque, the second-oldest in Cairo, dates from 990 though it was renovated in the 1980s. The symmetry of the large central courtyard has a simple elegance. Plain outer walls give it the look of a fortress more than a place of worship. The huge square gates that flank it are more akin to Crusader structures since their primary function was to protect the city. Guards would regulate those who entered and departed. Look for the graffiti of Napoleon's French soldiers on the stone of the towers; they spent some time garrisoned at the mosque and made sure they left their marks for posterity.

The southern boundary of the market is marked by the **al-Ghuri complex** of three buildings, a mosque, a *madrasa* (Koranic school) and a *wikala* (an Ottoman word for *caravanserai* or rooming house). They were built at the beginning of the 16th century by Sultan al-Ghuri, the last Mameluke ruler, and his mausoleum at the heart of the development is now a cultural centre hosting regular performances of the Whirling Dervishes (who achieve religious ecstasy by circling around in continuous motion). The *wikala*, now fully restored, hosts an arts centre where you can view and buy pieces by local artists.

Cairo's oldest mosque can be found just east of the al-Ghuri complex. **Al-Azhar Mosque** (meaning "The Splendid") was finished in 972, though it has been expanded many times over the centuries, and its remarkable inner sanctuary now covers 10,360 sq metres (4,000 sq ft). From the outset it was a centre of culture and learning, arguably the first university in the world. It is still the foremost school of Islamic studies, attracting over 85,000 students from around the Middle East.

You can walk south along the narrow alleyway cutting the Al-Ghuri complex to reach **Bab Zuweila Gate**, once the lower entrance to the city. The huge round bastions topped by ornate 14th-century minarets of the **Al-Muayyad Mosque** (*b.* 1420) frame a tiny gate that was used as a permanent scaffold to hang criminals in years gone by.

A short stroll west (right) down Ahmed Maher Street from the gate leads to the **Museum of Islamic Art**, inaugurated in 1903 and featuring 23 halls of beautifully crafted objects. Each room concentrates on a separate skill revealing excellent examples of carved wood, ivory, ceramics and manuscripts. Elaborately decorated arms are also on display. If you intend to take home some souvenir Islamic crafts, this is a good place to learn about traditional materials, motifs and patterns.

South of the market region, a 30-minute walk or 10-minute taxi ride, is **The Citadel** (Al-Qal'a), a massive fortification built on high ground in the early 13th century to protect the city from Crusaders. Later it became the palace of the Mamelukes and was a British garrison during WWII. The size of a small village, the site now houses mosques, museums and cafés, and is a place where tourists and local people gather away from the noise and dust of the city. The centrepiece of the Citadel is the **Mosque of Mohammed Ali**, built between 1824 and 1857. The largest mosque in the city, it has earned the name "alabaster mosque" for its grand interior faced with the smooth pale stone. The inner sanctuary hall is a truly monumental space in Ottoman Turkish style, capped with a series of beautifully painted domes. The tomb of Mohammed Ali sits under the colonnade. Its Carrera marble façade is incised with intricate carvings of traditional Islamic themes. Next to the Mosque of Mohammed Ali is the much simpler **el-Nasir Mosque**, with a small inner courtyard.

You'll be able to explore the **Military Museum** and **Carriage Museum** during your tour, but do take time to visit the vantage points along the western wall for wonderful views down onto vast areas of the Citadel and panoramic views across Cairo.

The minarets that you see in the foreground belong to two important Islamic buildings. On the left is the **Madrasa of Sultan Hasan**, built in 1362. There are in fact four separate schools within the structure and each one has its own portal and inner courtyard. The original minaret on the southwest corner is the tallest in Cairo at 81 metres (265 ft). To the

The Coptic Museum, Old Cairo's biggest attraction, covers every aspect of Coptic art and religion.

right of the *madrasa* is the **Al-Rafai Mosque**, completed in 1902 and the last greatest religious structure to be built in the city. It forms the resting places of many lesser members of the house of Mohammed Ali, and is where the last Shah of Iran was interred following his death in 1980.

A short walk west from the Citadel leads to the **Mosque of Ibn Tulun**, founded in 876 as the religious centre of a great military compound established by Ibn Tulun who was appointed governor of Egypt in 868. The mosque is unusual in Cairo in that it has no façade – it is hidden behind a protective wall with 19 openings. It also has the only spiral minaret in the city.

The **Gayer-Anderson Museum** beside Ibn Tulun Mosque was built as a private residence in 1540 and amalgamated with a neighbouring house called the House of the Cretan Woman (Bayt al-Kritliya) dating from 1631. British army office Robert Gayer-Anderson bought the latter between the two World Wars, and fully restored it with exquisite fretwork, wooden balconies, tiled floors and simple stucco walls. The museum displays the outstanding Islamic and European furniture, art and handicrafts collected by Gayer-Anderson during his time in Egypt.

Old Cairo

In the early years of Christianity, a strong church – the Coptic – was established in Egypt, and it flourished in this area, now south of the city centre. The church has survived to the present day. Almost nine percent of Egyptians are Christian.

To reach Old Cairo take the Nile River Bus from the jetty near the Ramses Hilton Hotel; it will drop you at the terminus of Masr El-Qadeema. Or take the metro line 1 to Mari Girgis Station.

Enter Old Cairo by the old Roman Gate – the Romans established a fort here following their annexation of the country – where you will find a concentration of Coptic churches and monasteries. The 7th-century **El Moallaqah** or "Hanging Church" gets its name from its location – it was built between two towers of the Roman gate and claims to be the oldest church in Egypt because its foundations date from the 4th century AD. Nearby **Abu Serga Church** (St. Sergius) also claims this distinction; it is said to have been built at the site where Joseph, Mary and the infant Jesus took shelter after they fled to Egypt from the Holy Land.

The **Church of Saint Barbara** is also worth visiting; it is typically Coptic in style. Next door is the **synagogue Ben-Ezra**, now no longer used for regular services, though the guardian will allow you to look inside if he is available.

The main attraction in Old Cairo is the **Coptic Museum**. Housed in an old *byat*, it is currently under renovation, but the work is mostly on the exterior leaving the wealth of artefacts

St. Sergius church, in the Coptic area, has special Christian significance.

In Giza, camels and their riders pause for a break at the base of the Great Pyramid of Cheops.

inside undisturbed. The collection covers all aspects of Coptic art and worship, from vestments, tapestries, early handwritten Bibles and painted icons, to ornate stone niches and wood-carved ceilings taken from churches all across Egypt. The guardians are particularly helpful and attentive.

The Pyramids

Giza

The pyramids of Egypt have exerted a powerful hold on the world since explorers first began to examine this ancient land in detail. Were they simply tombs for pharaohs, or astronomical markers to aid the quantifying of time; or were they built to concentrate a natural energy source? More outlandish theorists posit that the pyramids were not built by humans at all, speculating that they are a sign of an alien intelligence, which visited the earth many thousands of years ago.

Whatever the latest theory, the Pyramids of Giza (the most well-known) are, without doubt, an amazing sight as you stand before them. Their sandstone façades reflect the sunlight: rose-coloured in the morning, golden in the heat of the day, and smoky purple as night falls. One can't fail to marvel at the feat of engineering and organisation that resulted in millions of individual stone blocks being transported to the site and placed precisely one atop another with very little error in alignment, all without the aid of power tools or lifting equipment.

Archaeologists have concluded that the Giza pyramids were built within a few hundred years of each other by generations of the same royal family *circa* 2600 BC as elaborate tombs designed to foil robbers. The largest of the three, the **Great Pyramid of Cheops**, is the only survivor of the "Seven Wonders of the World" described by Greek and Roman scholars. It stands 137 metres (450 ft) high and was the tallest structure in the world until the building of the Eiffel Tower in Paris in 1898. Originally capped with a smooth layer of limestone, it would have reflected sunlight like a beacon across the Nile valley. The interior could not be more in contrast to the vast exterior. Steep, narrow tunnels lead to a tiny funerary chamber furnished by a simple granite sarcophagus. Look for the ventilation shafts that astronomers have proved aligned with major constellations in the skies of Ancient Egypt.

The **Pyramid of Chephren** is smaller than the Great Pyramid, though its location on slightly higher ground makes it appear taller. The interior chamber was found to contain a red granite sarcophagus. The smallest pyramid, that of **Mykerinus**, adds a wonderful perspective to the panorama, particularly when you align the pyramids for that souvenir photograph. To the south of this are three smaller, unfinished pyramids thought to be for the family of Mykerinus.

These three now-famous pharaohs were not the only ones laid to rest here however. Giza was the site of a royal burial ground from the days of the Early Empire, and the desert landscape is dotted with numerous mud-brick tombs and *mastabas* (stone tombs with flat roofs), though they are not as impressive as the pyramids themselves.

Standing at the base of the sacred causeway that once linked the pyramids to the Nile is the **Sphinx**, the enigmatic depiction of Chephren with his head attached to a lion's body. Sphinxes were guardian deities in Egyptian mythology and this was monumental protection, standing 73 metres (240 ft) long and 20 metres (66 ft) high. Following Chephren's death the body of the Sphinx was lost under the desert sands that swept the

The Sphinx stands guard before the Great Pyramid.

area and Tutmosis IV believed that the statue spoke to him, telling him he would become pharaoh if he cleared the sand away. Following this, ancient Egyptians believed that the monument possessed prophetic powers, and it still has a mysterious hold on the modern psyche.

The most recent attraction at the pyramid complex is a small museum housing the remains of a **solar barque** (a cedar longboat) which was found in 1954. The boat was made to carry the spirit of Chephren into the Other World after his death.

You can tour the pyramids on foot, or take a camel or horseback ride between the main sites. Many people choose to embark on the longer journey on horseback to view the monuments in a serene and timeless fashion.

Once you've seen the real thing, you may want to visit **The Pharaonic Village**, a theme park recreating life in Ancient Egypt. Colourful temples are presided over by priests, and reed boats ply the waterways in this interesting park that will certainly help children understand how ancient peoples may have lived – it may also help the adults. There's a good re-creation of King Tutankhamun's tomb at the time of its discovery, so you can see just how it looked to Howard Carter in 1922. The park also has a restaurant and children's play area.

Saqqara

☛ Giza was not the only location where pyramids were built – there are many archaeological sites scattered throughout the Western Desert – and it was not the place where pyramid-building started. To see the first and oldest pyramid you must make an hour's journey to the south of Cairo to Saqqara, and, following this, on to the ancient capital of Lower Egypt – Memphis.

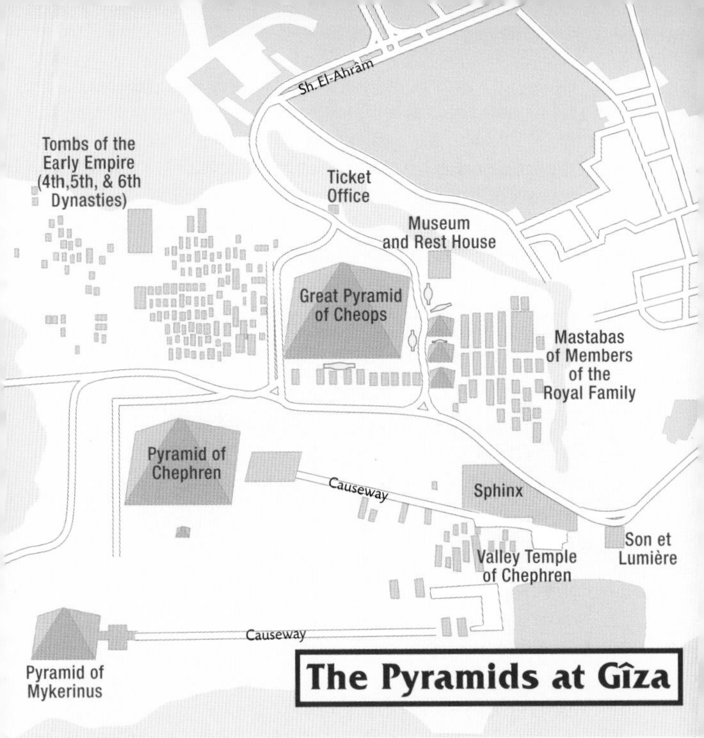

The Pyramids at Gîza

Saqqara was the final resting place for the rulers of Memphis and constitutes the largest royal graveyard in Egypt. Pride of place at the site is taken by the **Step Pyramid**, built by architect Imhotep for his ruler King Djoser *circa* 2670 BC. The pyramid is made up of six brick tiers, reaching a height of 60 metres (196 ft). Inside the structure a shaft was dug 28 metres (91 ft) into the bedrock where King Djoser's burial chamber was situated. The pyramid is surrounded by a compound designed to mimic the king's palace at his court in

Memphis, with beams, columns and bundles of reeds carved onto its façade. Several tombs surrounding the pyramid have extremely fine murals, particularly **Mereruka's tomb** (2300 BC), the largest yet discovered at the site, and **Ti's tomb**, with murals of fish and birds. The **Mastaba of Princess Idut** has exceptional nautical scenes and you'll also catch sight of the name of a tomb robber – Ahmed the Carpenter – who couldn't resist letting the world know about his visit.

The Essence of Egyptian Mythology

The god Ra was the primal creator deity, controlling everything in the universe. Ra begat four children: Shu and Tefnut, who became the atmosphere; Keb, who became the earth; and Nut who became the sky.

In the second generation, Keb and Nut had two sons, Set and Osiris, and two daughters, Isis and Nepthys. Osiris took the role of king of the earth and married his sister Isis. Set was jealous of his brother and killed him, chopping up his body and scattering the parts across the land. Isis set out to look for her husband/brother and found all the pieces apart from his genitals. With the help of Anubis, god of the dead, Isis embalmed Osiris and in his mummified state he fathered a son, Horus, through a mystical ritual performed by Isis. Osiris then became king of the underworld and of male fertility, with Horus taking on the role of king of the Earth. Horus, at the same time, took vengeance on Set, killing his uncle after an extremely bloody fight.

Of the once-white walls of **Memphis**, little remains, but it was capital of Egypt until the end of the Sixth Dynasty (*circa* 2200 BC). The two major relics are a monumental statue of Ramses II lying prostrate after losing its feet, and an alabaster sphinx dating from 1400 BC.

ALEXANDRIA AND THE MEDITERRANEAN COAST

There are two roads from Cairo to Alexandria. One leads through the fertile lands of the Nile Delta, past fields of cotton, rice, and numerous fruits and vegetables. Life seems to

The fort of Qait Bey watches over the harbour entrance, and houses the interesting Naval Museum.

have changed little in generations, though the mud-brick houses now have the benefit of electricity. The second route leads out through the desert to the west of Cairo on a new four-lane highway that leads to Wadi Natrun.

Wadi Natrun was one of the most important areas of Egypt in ancient times, primarily because it was the main source of natron, the mineral used in the mummification and glassmaking processes. Coptic Christians founded an expansive community for prayer and contemplation here in the 4th-century AD when many monks chose to live their lives as hermits.

Four monasteries, developed as a source of protection, still remain, and each has a church, monks' quarters and a sturdy high wall. **Deir Abu Maker** is the most important, having provided several leaders for the Coptic church; nearby is **Deir Anba-Baramos**. **Deir Es-Suryani**, as the name suggests, was a community of Syrian monks and its neighbour, **Deir Anba Bishoi**, is of typical design with a tiny round-domed 4th-century church and inner defensive bastion dating from the 9th century. Holy Mass is said daily in the Coptic language but an English-speaking priest is available to give you a comprehensive guided tour.

Alexandria

Founded by Alexander the Great on the Mediterranean coast in 322 BC, Alexandria was capital of Egypt during the Ptolemaic era. It was a city of beautiful palaces and temples, and a place of learning, with one of the most renowned libraries in the world. Ships from around the Mediterranean docked at the double harbour. The harbour's entrances were protected by the **Pharos Lighthouse**, one of the Seven Wonders of the World. Unfortunately, all this was lost in a series of earthquakes in the early centuries of the first millennium and Ancient Alexandria now rests below the waters of today's harbour. Recent underwater archaeological excavations have revealed a wealth of stone blocks and statuary lying only a few feet below the surface.

Although ancient Alexandria sank into the sea, the city continued to flourish as a trading port. It was the main entry point into Egypt until the advent of air travel in the early 20th century and its contact with a range of international influences made it the most cosmopolitan city in Egypt. Throughout the late 19th and early 20th centuries it was home to numerous British "ex-pats," one of whom, the writer Lawrence Durrell, painted a graphic picture of European life here. However, the climate changed after the 1952 coup and today, though you can still discern the European feel of Alexandria, there is no doubt that it is an Egyptian city.

The city sits on a wide bay with the colonial sandstone apartments on the waterside making a wonderful panorama as the sun begins to drop in the afternoons. Myriad fishing boats bob in the water, their catches making the short journey across the wide **corniche** to supply the day's menus at local seafood restaurants. The western end of the bay sweeps round to a headland, which is thought to be the location for the famous Alexandria Lighthouse. Today, the 15th century **Fort of Qait Bey** watches over the harbour entrance. It houses the Naval Museum with a collection of relics from the French Naval sojourn here in 1798. Just west of the fort is the former royal **palace of Ras El-Tin**, built for Mohammed Ali in 1834. It was here in 1952 that King Farouk signed his abdication before boarding his yacht for exile in Italy.

You can walk back to the centre of town along the corniche. It takes around 30 minutes and is a very pleasant stroll thanks to the cool breezes that come off the sea. Look

Deir Anba Bishoi, one of four monasteries founded by Coptic Christians in Wadi Natrun.

for the elaborate Oriental lines of the **Mosque of Abu El Abbas** on your right. Rebuilt in 1943, it holds the tombs of the 18th-century sheikh and other nobles. Take time to explore the exquisite Moorish stonework and the elegant domes and minaret.

A small square on the seafront marks the centre of town. Mini-buses dart in and out of the traffic to pick up passengers and there's a frantic rush at peak times as everyone tries to leave the city at once. Look for the **Cecil Hotel** on the western end of the square. Once the gathering place of the colonial "glitterati", it still draws European travellers for a glimpse of a genteel past.

Take a right at the square and walk away from the seafront past the tram terminus that links eastern Alexandria with the city centre. Off El Hurriya Street you'll find the Neo-Classical façade of the **Greco-Roman Museum** with a fine collection of Roman, Greek and Ptolemaic artefacts found around the city and under the waters of the harbour, along with many ancient Egyptian pieces. There is a marble statue of Julius Caesar, consort of Queen Cleopatra, who spent many months here, and a bust of Alexander, which was carved in his likeness after his death.

South of the museum and surrounded by modern housing lie the **Roman Baths**. Built in the 3rd-century AD, they played host to those in the upper echelons of Roman Alexandria who would come to the baths to relax and exchange news whilst enjoying a soak or a massage. A little

The skyline of cosmopolitan Alexandria makes for a striking view at sunset.

further southwest are some 2nd-century AD catacombs with tomb chambers painted to depict Greco-Egyptian themes.

Pompey's Pillar sits only a few minutes' walk to the southwest. The 30-metre (95-ft) high Corinthian column hewn from red granite stands on the site of the ancient Temple of Serapis. It was raised to honour Emperor Diocletian, not the Roman general that now gives the pillar its name.

The ancient library of Alexandria, founded by Ptolemy I, was said to be the greatest collection of manuscripts in the ancient world, comprising some 70,000 items. Unfortunately, it was damaged by fire several times and what remained was completely destroyed in 640 during the Arab invasion. As the 20th century neared its end the Egyptian government sought to revive Alexandria as a centre of learning and recreate the **Alexandria Library**. With the help of UNESCO a new high-tech depository has been built on a site on the corniche, east of the central square. Its *avant-garde* circular design contrasts sharply with the dreary buildings around it. Clad with grey Aswan granite, it is engraved with letters and graphic inscriptions of cultures and societies around the world. The library will house over 4 million volumes composed of books, tapes, maps, videos and discs.

The city of Alexandria has no proper beaches but 8 km (5 miles) to the east is **Montazah**, a resort centre with hotels and sandy bays. **Montazah Palace**, built in the 19th century as a hunting lodge, started the fashion. It is now a smart hotel and casino surrounded by beautiful gardens.

The Mediterranean Coast

West of Alexandria, civilisation gives way to empty desert except along the coast, where the late 1990s saw a building boom. Where only recently there were virgin beaches, now mile upon mile of concrete holiday complexes line the strand until you reach **El-Alamein**, a 90-minute drive along the coast. This tiny desert railway crossing was the scene of one of the pivotal battles of WWII, where Allied soldiers defeated Rommel's German and Italian forces in 1942. The military cemeteries of both the sides engaged in the historical battle now stand as a poignant memorial to the death and destruction that took place in the heat of the desert. There is also a small museum here with uniforms, military hardware and maps illustrating the battle plans and tactics of this most gruelling theatre of war.

UPPER EGYPT

The land of Upper Egypt sits in the south of the country, and it takes its name because it is upriver of the Cairo and Nile Delta area, which are known as Lower Egypt. Upper Egypt was the heartland of the kingdom at the peak of its power and influence, and the remains of its ancient cities form one of the most important and breathtaking archaeological collections in the world.

Luxor and the Valley of the Kings

The modern town of Luxor is one of two towns forming tourist bases on the Nile Valley. Its name in Arabic – El-Uqsor – means "gods' palaces", and it indicates the supreme importance of this area to the Ancient Egyptians. Luxor (known to the Ancient Greeks as Thebes) was for many centuries the capital city and religious focal point of Egypt.

The modern town sits on the east bank of the Nile some 800 km (500 miles) from Cairo. Thebes reached it peak in the New Kingdom era (*circa* 1540–1100 BC). By the time the Romans arrived it was already in decline, having lost influence when Assyrian raiders seized control in the 7th-century

The avenue of Ram-Headed Sphinxes at the Karnak Temple.

BC and the Ptolemaic leaders made their base at Alexandria in the 4th-century BC. In the following centuries sand swept through the area burying many of the buildings. The Arab town was erected atop this sandy layer and many treasures are still lost below the surface of the modern streets. In the past hundred years, Luxor's major historic buildings have been cleared of sand allowing visitors to view the temple structures. Across the river on the west bank are the remains of other temples, and more importantly, the burial places of the great pharaohs of Ancient Egypt, hidden in a slender valley beyond the narrow fertile river plain.

In the heart of the modern town, set beside the waters of the Nile, is **Luxor Temple**, started by Amenophis III in the 18th Dynasty (*circa* 1350 BC) and embellished by Ramses II in the 19th Dynasty. The temple served a specific purpose: to host the New Year celebration to the God Amun who would be represented in both his positive form, Amun Ra – the sun god, and his negative form, Amun-Min – a lustful, wanton and outrageous demon.

The great pylon (the grand entranceway with twin towers) of the temple is fronted by majestic statues of Ramses II and a large granite obelisk – once one of a pair (the other was presented to the French government by Mohammed Ali and now graces the Place de la Concorde in Paris). Before heading into the inner sanctum of the temple, stride along the **Avenue of Ram-Headed Sphinxes**, which points in the direction of Karnak Temple *(see page 53)* to the north. These were erected by Nectanebo during the 4th-century BC.

Entering the main courtyard of the temple, you will find a peristyle hall (with one row of supporting columns) decorated with fluted columns that were commissioned by Queen Hatshepsut, and several impressive statues of Ramses II fashioned from black and red granite. Perhaps the most fascinating element of the hall is the **Mosque of Abu El Haggag**, which was built within the temple complex to protect the tomb of a 12th-century descendant of Mohammed's brother-in-law. The mosque and tomb were erected on the

Tutankhamun and his wife grace Luxor Temple.

bed of sand that covered the temple and now sit 5 metres (20 ft) or so above the excavated floor level. The entrance to the mosque is through a door in the east wall above the temple complex.

As you move further into the complex, look for statues of **King Tutankhamun and his wife**, one of few depictions of the young boy pharaoh to be found at his capital. From the hall, a colonnade leads to an immense hypostyle (with columns supporting the roof) hall, decorated with double rows of papyrus columns with beautifully preserved colours, and on to the **Court of Amenophis III**. Elaborate carvings on the walls of both buildings depict Amenophis making offerings to the gods in thanks for his divine power.

Luxor temple does not have a sound and light show but it is open late each evening, offering you a chance to enjoy the majestic remains under floodlights – a very romantic sight to behold.

Between Luxor Temple and the Nile is the **corniche**, a tree-lined avenue carrying traffic through the town and officially called El-Nil Street. A wide riverside walkway allows you to stroll and benches allow for a shady seat. Here, the *felucca* (Nile sailboat) pilots gather, trying to sell an afternoon or sunset trip on their graceful craft, and Nile Cruisers lie several abreast, disgorging their passengers for tours or shopping trips. Horse-drawn carriages ply the corniche offering trips to Karnak, or a ride back to your hotel.

Also on the riverside of El-Nil Street is the **Mummy Museum**, with an eclectic collection of artefacts and information about the art of mummification. The "official" **Archaeological Museum of Luxor** lies a little way north. The modern air-conditioned building is well designed, with a small number of delightful pieces on display including a striking basalt statue of Pharaoh Tutmosis III.

North of Luxor temple, in the streets behind the Mosque of Abu El Haggag, is the bustling **souk** or market where you'll find a mixture of tourist souvenirs and local products such as food or textiles. Browsing is difficult as vendors are attentive and can be insistent, but you'll have fun. If you want to buy pottery or alabaster, compare prices and quality with goods on sale at the artisan villages on the west bank before making a final decision.

The **Temple of Karnak** sits in the northern half of the town of Thebes (No-Amun or "the City of Amun" in ancient Egyptian) now 2 km (1½ miles) from modern Luxor. Begun during the Old Kingdom, it was the national shrine of the country (the "St. Peter's" of Ancient Egyptian religion) from the 11th Dynasty period, *circa* 2134 BC. The temple complex was expanded over subsequent centuries, with each generation adding their own shrines and monuments. During excavations, a cache of 17,000 items dating from the Roman era was found. It was finally abandoned towards the 4th-century AD when the country looked to a new group of deities.

The largest temple in Egypt, the site extends over 3 sq km (1 sq mile). Standing at the heart of the complex is the **Temple of Amun**, greatest of all Theban gods. This monumental construction covers a 140-sq-metre (1,500-sq-ft) area, with a hypostyle hall, consisting of 122 columns in nine rows, 21 metres (70 ft) high, which is considered to be one of the finest ancient structures in the country.

The avenue of the ram-headed sphinxes flanks the route from the Nile to the temple entrance. This was used for ceremonial purposes, allowing statues of the gods to be carried to the river for journeys to the west bank, or to the Luxor sanctuary. Karnak was linked to Luxor Temple by a 2-km (¾-mile) avenue decorated with smaller temples and flanked by sphinxes, most of which now lie below the modern streets.

From the ticket office you enter the temple complex through a colossal pylon, one of the most recent structures at the site and the largest constructed anywhere in Egypt during the Ptolemaic period. However, the structure was never finished and lacks the epic reliefs (carved images) found at Philae and Denderah *(see pages 70 and 62).*

Walk through the gateway and you'll find yourself in an immense open space – the largest temple courtyard in the country. To the left is the diminutive **Temple of Seti II**, and further along on the right a larger **temple dedicated to Ramses III**. A second smaller pylon, fronted by statues of Ramses II, shields Karnak Temple's greatest architectural masterpiece – the **Great Hypostyle Hall**. Its immense columns (the top of each one could accommodate 50 standing children) recreate the papyrus forests of the sacred island from which all life sprang (also representing the landscape of Lower Egypt), and they were highly decorated and brilliantly painted in their heyday.

A third pylon leads on to the oldest parts of the temple, past obelisks added at the behest of Pharaoh Seti I and Queen Hatshepsut in the New Kingdom era. The pink granite "needle" of the queen is the tallest in Egypt, pointing 30 metres (97 ft) into the sky. It was originally topped by a cap of pure gold, which reflected the bright sunlight and acted as a beacon for those who searched from afar for the temple. Look for a simple statue of Tutankhamun, the boy king, below the needle. He consolidated power at Ancient Thebes during his short reign.

Beyond the main temple complex, Karnak stretches out over the landscape as far as the eye can see, but many of the other remains are more difficult to identify. An interesting building towards the rear is the **Festival Hall of Tutmoses III**. It recreates in stone the field tent the pharaoh used when on military campaigns, with the central row of columns higher than the outer, meant to hold an imaginary canvas high above the head.

South of the main temple complex you will find the **Sacred Lake**, used in ceremonial processions. Today it forms the foreground for the seated part of the Sound and Light Show. Stop at the giant granite **scarab** on the north-west corner of the lake. When Amunophis III originally commissioned the scarab it was placed at his temple on the west bank. Egyptians consider it lucky to walk three times counter-clockwise around the scarab before touching it and making a wish.

The Theban Necropolis and the Valley of the Kings

While ruling from palaces on the east bank of the Nile, pharaohs chose to be buried on the west bank, as this was the last resting place of the god Amun Ra, in the form of the setting sun. Tuthmosis I was the first pharaoh to be entombed there *circa* 1490 BC, choosing a narrow valley out of site of the capital as a secret

This Colossus of Memnon once guarded a temple that no longer exists.

and supposedly safe location for his resting place, cut deep into the rock. Numerous other rulers followed him, creating a veritable "city of the dead" with each tomb more elaborate or brightly decorated than the last.

Though the Valley of the Kings has become popularly known, it is not the only ancient attraction on the west bank of the Nile. There are temples, towns and hundreds of other tombs of lesser though important mortals such as high priests, nobles and highly regarded artisans who worked on the royal tombs. The tombs are known collectively as the Theban Necropolis.

From the ferry docking station on the west bank, head to the nearby ticket office where you can purchase tickets for all the separate archaeological sites. From there, the road leads directly towards the range of low hills that hide the tombs. You'll pass two huge sentinel statues 21 metres (68 ft) high on the river plain facing out towards the Nile. These are the **Colossi of Memnon**, statues of Pharaoh Amenophis III that once guarded the entrance to his temple, which has now completely disappeared.

At the split in the roadway, a left turn will lead you directly to the **Valley of the Queens**, and the temple complex of **Medinet Habu**. Often left out of the tour group itinerary, this part of the west bank can be much quieter than the better-known attractions, but it offers some interesting insights into Egyptian life and some excellent remains. Queens and royal children were buried in a valley separate from their respective fathers and husbands. The renowned Theban queen Nefertari, wife of Ramses II, has the most ornate tomb (number 66), although unfortunately it is not always accessible.

Below the Valley of the Queens are the remains of the town of the artisans, called **Deir el-Medina**. This is the settlement where the generations of painters, masons and builders who worked on the royal tombs lived. Simple brick homes stand row upon row and archaeologists found a wealth of everyday artefacts from cooking utensils to work tools, painting a vivid picture of the ancients' activities. Archaeologists also discovered a number of simple tombs where the artisans buried their dead. Brightly decorated by their peers, they depict the incumbent in life, at work or labouring in the fields. Both the **Tomb of Sennedjem** (number 1) and **Innerkhau** (number 359) are worth exploring.

A right turn at the junction leads along the valley floor past the modern artisan village of **Sheik Abd el-Gurnah**, where you will be able to buy alabaster and onyx pieces. The simple brick buildings faced with ochre and blue stucco, though larger than those at Deir el-Medina, are little changed in style. There are a number of tombs and temples scattered in farmland here; the most prominent is the mortuary temple of Ramses II, the **Ramesseum**. Built to hold festivities during his visits from Thebes, the Ramesseum was decorated with majestic statues of the pharaoh, and the pylon depicts him triumphant at the Battle of Qadesh when he quashed the Hittites. Unfortunately, much of the temple lies in ruins.

Tombs of the Nobles sit between the Ramesseum and the village. The best of these date back to the 18th Dynasty when Egyptian art and creativity were at their peak. Take time to explore number 52, the **Tomb of Nacht**, a temple astronomer. The paintings that cover the walls depict the Nile at its most splendid, with abundant fruit and depictions of wine-making. The nearby **Tomb of Mena** (number 69) is also worth a visit for realistic scenes of harvesting and threshing. **Tomb 57**, that of Khaemhat, was decorated with statues of himself and his family – very rare for tombs of his class. **Ramose's Tomb** is also important: a high official in the court of Amenophis IV,

At the Temple of Denderah, a bust of goddess Hathor.

he began to prepare an elaborate resting place decorated with fine bas-reliefs. The tomb was abandoned when Amenophis left Thebes and made a new capital at Tell el-Amarna to the north. Ramose dutifully followed his master there to engage in an experimental new way of living.

Before turning off the coastal plain into the Valley of the Kings, one of the most impressive Theban temples comes into view on the left, that of Queen Hatshepsut. She was a remarkable woman, gaining power as regent for the young Tutmosis II – her stepson – before usurping it for herself by claiming divine right to rule. The **Temple of Hatshepsut**, dedicated to the goddess Hathor, is a vast three-tiered structure carved into the base of the rose-coloured hillside facing out towards the river. Each level has a colonnaded façade, and as you approach on foot it gives you the opportunity to take in the monumental scale.

The Lower Terrace is cut by a wide ramp leading to a large courtyard at Middle Terrace level and a smaller ramp leading to the Upper Terrace (unfortunately closed to visitors).

Behind the colonnades on the **Middle Terrace**, located to the left of the ramp, are carved scenes depicting a trade mission bringing myrrh and incense from Egypt's neighbour Punt, present-day Somalia. A small temple to Hathor situated to the left of the colonnade has columns carved with the cow's head that depicted her. To the right the walls are carved with scenes from the life of Queen Hatshepsut, including her divine birth, where her mother is shown being attended by Heket, the frog-headed midwife god, watched over by Amun himself. Anubis (God of Mummification) has a small temple here and you will clearly see his jackal-headed form on the walls.

Many carvings of Hatshepsut at the temple have been defaced. In fact, Tutmosis II tried to remove all traces of her at Luxor and Karnak when he finally became pharaoh following her death, but this does not spoil the formidable architectural achievement of the temple itself.

The **Valley of the Kings** lies out of view in the hills behind Hatshepsut's Temple. As you turn to head up into the valley, look for a house on the left surrounded by shady trees. This was the field base for Howard Carter during the long search that finally resulted in the finding of Tutankhamun's treasure-filled tomb.

Tickets for the Valley of the Kings allow you to visit three tombs, so if you want to visit more you must buy several tickets. There are over 60 tombs in the valley – and some yet to be discovered – dating from *circa* 1490–1100 BC, but not all will be open on your visit. The most impressive and important are listed below.

The **Tomb of Tutankhamun** (number 62) is without doubt the most famous, but the interior is disappointing. The king died very young and artisans had only just begun to dig the chambers, so it's small and sparsely decorated. Undoubtedly the discovery of an undisturbed tomb and its vast treasure trove in 1922 is what maintains its popularity.

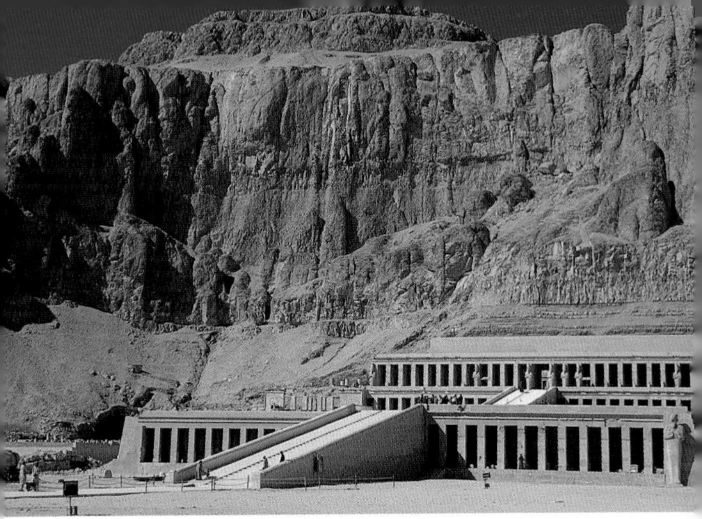

One of the most impressive of the Theban temples is that of Queen Hatshepsut, honouring the cow goddess Hathor.

Also, the king's mummy is the only one still in situ – many others are on display in the Egyptian Museum in Cairo *(see page 26)*. There is an extra fee to enter the tomb.

Other tombs in the valley are much more instructive about Egyptian life, death and the afterlife. They are also larger and more brilliantly decorated.

The **Tomb of Ramses VI** (9) reopened in 2000 after major renovations. The long tomb shaft is decorated with excellent paintings depicting chapters of the Book of the Dead – the rituals to be performed for Egyptians to reach the afterlife.

The **Tomb of Seti I** (17), *circa* 1279 BC, is one of the largest in the valley, and has some of the finest decoration. There are five connecting corridors, two pits and four rooms before the burial chamber is reached. The king pays his respects to the deities, including Ra and Kephri, as he makes his symbolic journey.

In *circa* 1151, masons dug a shaft 10 metres (33 ft) into the bedrock for **Ramses III's tomb** (11). The corridors then continue 125 metres (410 ft) to the burial chamber. Look for scenes of boats sailing on the Nile, and weapons of war including spears and shields. Two harpists sing the praises of Ramses before the deities, giving rise to the temple's alternative name – Temple of the Harpists.

Ramses IV was responsible for saving many of the mummies of his ancestors after tomb robbers desecrated their places of rest, stealing the treasures without thought for the reputation of the dead rulers. He organised the rewrapping of many mummies and devised a secret hiding place for them in a narrow valley behind the Temple of Hatshepsut. His tomb has good wall reliefs protected by glass screens.

A splendid red granite sarcophagus has pride of place in the **Tomb of Horemheb**; you'll need to walk down a long steep corridor to reach it. Ninety steps will lead you down to the depths of the **Tomb of Amenophis II** (35); it is the deepest in the valley. Several mummies were found here when archaeologists opened it, leading to a much-improved understanding of the genealogy of the various dynasties.

One of the most remote tombs is that of **Tutmosis III** (34; *circa* 1425 BC), in the far west of the valley, which rewards the intrepid wanderer. A rickety flight of steps links with the tomb entrance before you make your way down inside to the ornate burial chamber. As you descend, look for images of over 700 deities decorating the walls before reaching the chamber with its finely carved red sandstone sarcophagus; a royal *cartouche* (hieroglyphic nameplate) above the lintel heralds your arrival. Tutmosis chose the location of his tomb well for it was not totally robbed in antiquity and numerous

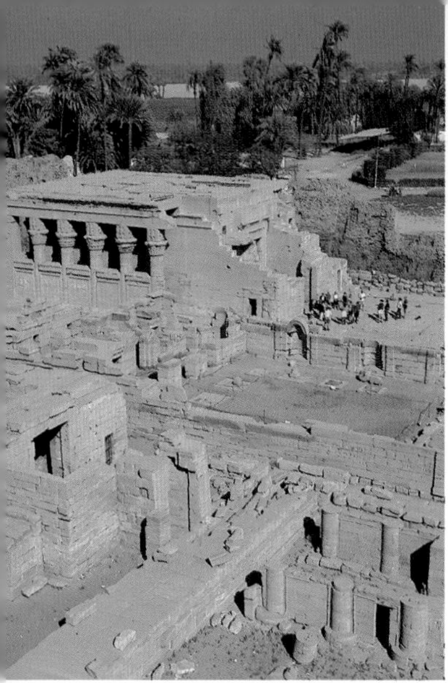

Overview of the Temple of Denderah complex.

artefacts found in the antechambers are now on show in the Egyptian Museum in Cairo *(see page 26).*

North of Luxor

Though independent travel is difficult north of Luxor because of security precautions put in place to protect tourists *(see DRIVING, page 111)*, there are still two temple complexes that can be visited from your base at Luxor. Booking a tour is probably your easiest option.

The first is the **Temple of Denderah** some 60 km (43 miles) north. The major temple of the cow goddess Hathor, it was begun in the Ptolemaic era, *circa* 125 BC, making it one of the later Egyptian temples. It was a major centre of female deity worship in Upper Egypt at the time and the Ptolemaic Queen Cleopatra worshipped here. She, in turn, was worshipped by her subjects as a living goddess. There is a unique relief of the queen found on the rear façade of the temple, the only representation from her lifetime to have been identified. The Romans completed the temple in AD 60 and as you explore the interior you can see the *cartouches* of Roman emperors on the walls. Denderah also has excellent ceiling details, depicting goddess Nut on her journey across the sky, though they have been blackened by the fires of Coptic Christians and Arabs who later made the temple their home. If you are not claustrophobic, take the opportunity to enter the crypt below the temple floor, as the carvings here were never defaced and are still precise and clean. Then climb up to the roof and take in the splendid views of the surrounding complex and the magnificent Nile valley beyond.

North of Denderah is **Abydos**, 150 km (93 miles) from Luxor, and erected for the worship of Osiris, god of the Underworld. It was a major funerary site of the ancient Egyptian pharaohs (*circa* 3100–2755 BC) and early *mastabas* can be found all around the site. The primary place of worship was the **Temple of Seti I**, which even today is an impressive sight. Built of limestone, it honoured generations of rulers who had passed on into the afterlife. Though Seti commissioned the temple between 1291 and 1279 BC, the colonnaded courtyards and ramps on its façade were added by his son, Ramses II, who usurped his father, trying every way possible to excise his name from the temple walls.

Reliefs carved into the stone show Ramses being welcomed by the gods – particularly Osiris, Isis and Horus – featured on the colonnade of the second terrace. There are two hypostyle halls with well-preserved papyrus columns and in the Corridor of the Kings located in the southwest wing you will find 76 *cartouches* listing pharaohs throughout the ages.

South of Luxor

The Nile valley south of Luxor is home to three temple complexes. These form the major stops of a Nile cruise and are all visited by tour groups from bases at Luxor or from Aswan to the south.

The first, reached from Luxor, is **Esna**, 54 km (33 miles) by road. The modern Egyptian town has been built on top of much of the ancient site of the **Temple of Knum** – ram-headed god of creation and protector of the Nile's source – and only the hypostyle hall remains, set 9 metres (30 ft) below the surrounding houses. The hall, begun in the reign of Emperor Tiberius following the Roman takeover, has pleasing proportions and the interior is decorated with reliefs depicting Roman emperors dressed in pharaoh's garb and worshipping Knum.

Situated some 50 km (30 miles) further south is the **Temple of Edfu**, the second-biggest temple in Egypt, and one of the best-preserved. Dedicated to Horus – god incarnate in the ruling pharaoh – his granite falcon emblems guard the temple entrance. The outer pylon is majestic. At 79 metres (260 ft) wide and 36 metres (118 ft) high, it was built by the Ptolemies during a total reconstruction of the temple in 237–105 BC.

Edfu was built in the classic Egyptian style and was little changed following its rebuilding. Behind the pylon is a courtyard, followed by two hypostyle halls and a sanctuary. Around the whole structure is a retaining wall with a narrow corridor allowing visitors to explore the carvings on every exterior wall. Reliefs depict Ptolemaic pharaohs worshipping Horus, and the interior carvings of their food offerings are especially impressive. The back walls of the pylon have scenes of the yearly meetings of Horus and his consort Hathor, who travelled on a sacred *barque* (slender boat) from her temple at Denderah for the reunion on the Nile. For the people of Egypt this was a time of celebration and there were two weeks of exuberant dancing, processions and feasting. At the heart of the sanctuary, a small granite shrine once held the sacred *barque* of Horus himself. For graphic scenes of Horus' fight with his evil uncle Seth to avenge his father

Osiris, walk around the exterior of the temple to the west side, where the whole event is re-created. This one incident reveals the Egyptians' ultimate belief in achieving the victory of "Good over Evil" through conduct in day-to-day matters. The two were finely balanced.

The **Kom Ombo Temple** (Temple of Horus) lies closest to Aswan – some 60 km (37 miles) south of Edfu. Situated on a knoll by the side of the Nile with views both up and downstream, it has one of the prettiest settings of any temple in Egypt.

Kom Ombo is an unusual temple in that it is dedicated to two gods. Before the building of the Aswan Dam, the River Nile was home to many thousands of crocodiles, and some would gather on the muddy banks here to sun themselves. Egyptians revered the strong and patient creatures and Kom Ombo is dedicated to Sobek, the crocodile god. It is also dedicated to Horus, since Egyptians thought that this was the place where the final battle between Horus and Seth (in the form of a crocodile) took place.

As you enter the temple site you'll see a small room housing several mummified crocodiles worshipped at the site, though they do have a moth-eaten appearance. You'll also see reliefs of Sobek and Horus flanking the entrance. The main attraction of Kom Ombo is the vibrant colour still found on the columns in the hypostyle hall. All Egyptian temples would have been vividly coloured – much like the tombs in the Valley of the Kings – but little colour has survived on most of them due to the effects of thousands of years of strong sunlight, and also of smoke damage caused by fires when the temples were used as dwelling places. Within the temple itself the gods share hypostyle halls and an inner sanctum. Each pays tribute to the other in reliefs on the interior walls.

Aswan

Aswan, Egypt's southernmost town, has played an important role throughout its long history. It marked the ancient border with Nubia to the south and was the conduit for the camel caravan trade in African products such as gold, ivory and spices. The word *aswan* actually means "trade" or "market" in ancient Egyptian, signifying its pre-eminent activity. The town has a high percentage of Nubians in its population; these people, though fully integrated into Egyptian society, remain proud of their separate cultural identity.

Aswan became a backwater following the decline of the Egyptian Empire, far removed from power bases at Alexan-

The many-columned hypostyle hall of the Temple of Kom Ombo, dedicated to crocodile god Sobek and to Horus.

dria and Cairo. It began to feel the benefits of tourism as Luxor did in the days of the Grand Tour, but has been transformed with the building of the **Aswan High Dam**, only 10 km (6 miles) south of the town. Some 2,000 Soviet engineers arrived to help with the mammoth project to stem the annual floods that plagued the country, and provide hydroelectricity to power a growth in industry. Completed in 1972, it has achieved both, but the fertility of Egyptian farmland is falling as it lacks the yearly layer of fresh nutrients brought by the flood. A visit to the dam brings home the immense engineering feat and allows you to gaze out over Lake Nasser, created by the blocking of the river, which is now over 500 km (310 miles) in length, spanning the border with Sudan.

For the Ancient Egyptians, Aswan was the place where the yearly flood of the Nile began. They could not travel upriver because several sets of cataracts blocked passage and they were unaware that the waters travelled from the heartland of Africa. They worshipped the Nile as the nourisher of life and built temples here to the Nile god, Hapy, and the creator god, Knum. The town was also important for the pharaohs as it sat close to one of the largest sources of high-quality granite quarries in the country, providing stone for many of its finest temples. The huge blocks were hauled to the quaysides to be carried upriver. Today, a visit to the quarries, just outside town, reveals some of the secrets of how the ancient Egyptians worked the stone. A huge **unfinished obelisk** lies prone: the immense monument – it would have been the largest in Egypt had it been completed – fractured along a fault line and was abandoned in 1500 BC.

Downtown Aswan has a pleasant riverside **Corniche** where you can stroll and watch the world go by. At its southern end you'll find **The Old Cataract Hotel**, harking back to the days of Edwardian elegance. It has seen such illustrious guests as Winston Churchill and Agatha Christie, who wrote her thriller *Death on the Nile* while staying here. The river looks wonderful from its period terrace and flower-strewn gardens, and it's *de rigueur* to enjoy afternoon tea or a cocktail while admiring the view.

On the main road out of town to the south, only a few minutes' walk from the hotel, is the imposing **Nubian Museum.** With a research facility and library dedicated to promoting Nubian traditions such as dance and music, it also displays finds rescued from several archaeological sites that were subsequently flooded by the waters of Lake Nasser in the 1970s.

One of the great pleasures of a trip to Aswan is taking a **felucca** out onto the Nile. These traditional low-draughted craft ply effortlessly and quietly through the water. Their white sails make a beautiful sight, especially at sunset. You can make several separate trips to view all the attractions that the town has to offer, and you'll certainly get used to the slow pace of these windblown boats. On the west bank of the river – set in a desert landscape – is the 7th-century **Coptic monastery of St. Simeon**, now sadly in ruins, and the **Mausoleum of the Aga Khan** (1877–1957), spiritual leader of the Ismaili Muslim sect. From the ferry station on the west bank it's a 40-minute walk across the sand, though this is not recommended. You can take a taxi or try a camel ride – very appropriate given the terrain.

The two islands of the Nile offer contrasting attractions. The northernmost – **Kitchener Island** – mwas given as a gift to the British general of the same name after his victories in the Sudan in the late 19th century. It is also known as Botanical Island for the exotic gardens created there. This is an excellent place to come and sit in the shade among the fragrant blooms. South of Kitchener Island is **Elephantine Island**, home to the **Temple of Knum**. To honour the ram-headed god, Egyptians created a necropolis of mummified rams at the site, covering the animals' corpses with gold leaf. Today they are on view in the museum on site but their stone sarcophagi still lie in the temple complex. You can also view a Roman **Nileometer** carved in the rock; this measured the height of the river and helped the ancient priests to time the announcement of the Nile flood which initiated a movement of workers from the fields to community projects such as temple building. It was refurbished in the Victorian era but rendered useless by succeeding Nile dams.

The creation of **Lake Nasser** as a consequence of the building of the Aswan High Dam caused many social and political concerns, not least because the waters were due to overwhelm a number of important ancient monuments.

Here, a smattering of distinctive* feluccas *sit moored along the shore of Elephantine Island.

Audacious plans were announced to move three of the most important and recreate them on higher ground out of danger. The Egyptians asked for international help to fund the projects, and UNESCO stepped in to provide money.

The nearest temple to Aswan Town is Philae. Originally built on an island in the Nile, it was already semi-submerged following the building of the first Aswan Dam in 1900. It was important to find a new island location where they could recreate the site, and one was found only 300 metres (900 ft) north of the original setting. Some 40,000 blocks of stone had to be labelled, moved and re-erected before the transformation was complete so that you can take a short boat ride out to the island, and enjoy views of the approach to the temple, just as the ancients did.

Philae Temple was known as the "Pearl of Egypt" for its beauty and picturesque setting. Dedicated to Isis, and her main centre of worship, it was inaugurated in the 4th-century BC. Worship carried on here longer than in other pagan sites in Egypt, with texts stating that pilgrims came as late as the 4th-century AD. It was later converted into a Coptic Christian place of worship and their crosses can still be seen carved into the lintels and door frames. The main temple of Isis was expanded throughout its long lifetime. The impressive outer pylon was erected in the 2nd-century BC to surround the older inner sanctum. The agora-like **Hall of Nactenabo** (381–362 BC) stands in front of the pylon. Small shrines honouring local gods lead from the hall, and there is a temple to Imhotep, the great architect of the pyramids who was deified in the centuries after his death. Inside the temple is a small birthing chamber or *mammisi*, where carved reliefs depict Isis holding her new-born son Horus. A second inner pylon shows Ptolemy XIII paying homage to Isis, who is flanked by her husband Osiris and Horus.

The Romans were active worshippers at Philae even adding their own touches. The **Kiosk of Emperor Trajan**, a beautiful building with ornate floral capitals supported by elegant Corinthian columns, makes a striking contrast to the Egyptian temple designs. Philae has one of the most evocative sound and light shows in Egypt, so do try and make time to return in the evening to see it.

Abu Simbel

Considered one of the greatest architectural achievements of the Ancient Egyptians, the temple complex at Abu Simbel is also one of the most famous. Ramses II did not build it from stone but had it hewn into the cliffs of the Nile valley at a spot that stands only 7 km (4 miles) from the Sudan border, in the ancient land of Nubia. When Lake Nasser threatened

Intricate hieroglyphs festoon the main pylon at the Temple of Philae in Aswan.

The Oases of the Western Desert

Though much of western Egypt is featureless desert, there are still isolated pockets of fertile land. These oases offer a contrast to the dusty capital, or the Nile towns packed with tourists and traders. The local the people are Bedouins from Arabia, or Berbers from North Africa, both nomadic peoples who have chosen to settle in the oases, rear their animals, and grow crops at a guaranteed source of water. The towns have grown sizeable in the early years of the 21st century. You'll find hectares of apricots, dates and olives growing around the settlements, men working in the fields, and young people tending herds.

A two-hour drive across the Western Desert from Cairo is Fayyoum, where nearby Lake Qaroun was a favoured hunting area for King Farouk. Archaeological remains from Egyptian to the Roman era lie in the flat farmland.

Kharga oasis, west of Luxor, is served by an airport, but much of the town is disappointing. Head for the oldest part of town – Darb El Sindaliya – dating back to the 10th century. A centre of early Christian worship, Copts took up residence at the 500 BC Temple of Hibis in the 3rd-century AD. Their burial site at Bagawat is one of the oldest in the world with over 200 mud-brick tombs and chapels.

Further out into the desert, Dakhla oasis supports a population of over 70,000, with village settlements scattered across the landscape. Mut has a small ethnology museum displaying the tools and utensils used by many generations of nomadic herdsmen and farmers. Or explore the narrow alleys of Bagat with its whitewashed walls and low tunnels.

to flood the complex in the 1970s, engineers had the unenviable task of formulating a plan to save it and this they did with consummate skill. An artificial cliffside was created on higher ground, matching the old in height and alignment. The temple stones were then dismantled and moved into place within this hill recreating the old site exactly, including leaving old fallen pieces on the ground in the place where they were originally excavated.

When Ramses built these temples in the 13th-century BC, he was at the height of his power and was stamping his mark all around his kingdom. In addition to asserting his authority over this region, the temples were also used for the storage of gold and other precious cargos carried by caravan from central Africa.

The façade of the **Temple of Ramses II** is one of the most enduring images of Egypt and though you may have seen it in photographs, it is truly breathtaking in reality. The four monumental colossi of Ramses II that frame the entrance stand 20 metres (65 ft) high and they are aligned to face the rising sun, to be infused with the energy of the sun god each day. The pharaoh sits impassively, wearing the double crown signifying his control over both Upper and Lower Egypt. Standing at his feet are diminutive representations of his family. Reliefs carved on Ramses' thrones depict the Nile gods, and in a niche between the two central colossi is a small statue to the god Ra-Herekhty (Ra the sun god combined with Horus) with whom Ramses shares the temple.

The design of this temple did not incorporate a forecourt and so you enter directly into the **hypostyle hall**. Carvings on the columns show Ramses (in the form of Osiris) making offerings to the gods, but around the walls he is seen smiting his foes during battles in Syria and is depicted as returning in triumph with hundreds of Hittite prisoners. The inner sanctum of the temple was aligned so that the first rays of the sun on 21 February and 21 October would fall on the sacred *barque* deposited here and on the statues of four gods (Ptah, Amun, Ramses II and Ra-Herekhty), though scholars are still not sure what was so propitious about these dates.

Near to the temple of Ramses II is a smaller edifice, the **Temple of Nefertari**, dedicated to his beloved wife. She, too, is deified and in a façade of six colossi 11.5 metres (38 ft) high stands at equal height to her husband – a very rare honour for a consort in Egypt – though his statues outnumber hers by a ratio of 2:1, a more subtle indication of his supreme power.

The royal offspring can be seen in miniature at the feet of their parents. Within the complex, dedicated to Hathor – her "cows head" form decorates the columns of the hypostyle hall – is a sanctuary where Ramses and Nefertari made offerings to the gods, and one showing the pharaoh himself worshipping his deified wife.

Most people take the regular flights from Aswan to Abu Simbel – around 50 minutes – but the four-hour overland route offers a fascinating insight into life away from the big tourist towns of Egypt if you have more time.

THE RED SEA COAST AND THE SUEZ CANAL

After touring the hot and dusty archaeological sites of the Nile Valley, or tramping through the noisy streets of Cairo, the Red Sea coast makes a welcome contrast. With cooling sea breezes and good sandy beaches, it offers all the basic ingredients needed for a relaxing holiday; Egyptian hoteliers and restaurateurs are working hard to provide the rest. Until the early 1990s much of the coastline was undeveloped, but a rash of building projects creates an almost continuous ribbon all along the shoreline.

The most established town is **Hurghada**, whose small offshore islands sit among some of the best diving waters in the world. The SCUBA community made this remote settlement their own, but with the building of an airport in the 1990s, Hurghada has seen a great influx of holidaymakers from around Europe. Some of the recent development is rather unattractive, but there are a number of excellent resort hotels providing just about everything you could want for a beach holiday.

Situated at the northern tip of the Red Sea coast, where the continent of Africa meets the Sinai peninsula, is one of the greatest engineering feats of modern times, the **Suez Canal**. This manmade artery, linking the Mediterranean with the Red Sea and the Indian Ocean, allowed a much quicker journey time from Europe to the Middle East, India and the Far East when it was opened in 1869; it was a huge aid to the Western European powers in managing their expansive empires.

Though the advent of air travel negates the need for passengers to take a long sea journey, the Suez Canal is still important for cargo vessels, and watching a leviathan tanker travel sedately through the passage is an unreal experience; unless you actually stand beside the canal you can't see the water and they look as though they are simply floating along on the sand.

The Sinai

This remote easternmost part of Egypt is still sparsely populated, and in its recent history it has been a political pawn between Egypt and Israel. Its northern deserts were a battleground in the Egypt-Israeli conflicts of the 1950s and

1960s, and it was occupied by Israel for many months before it passed permanently back into Egypt's hands with the treaty of 1979.

The Sinai is a wild and dramatically beautiful land pointing south out into the Red Sea. Although flat and monotonous sandy desert in the north, it rises in ranges of sandstone peaks in the south creating a strong contrast with the azure blue of the surrounding seas. Ancient seismic activity forced the stratified rock towards the sky and the action of wind and frost have fashioned it into bizarre shapes. Very little flourishes here – perhaps a solitary acacia tree whose roots seek water deep below the surface – but the odd desert fox will raise its long ears above the skyline, and you'll still see family groups of wild camels eking out an existence. The Sinai

The coastline of Hurghada have beautiful, sweeping beaches, and some of the best waters for diving in the world.

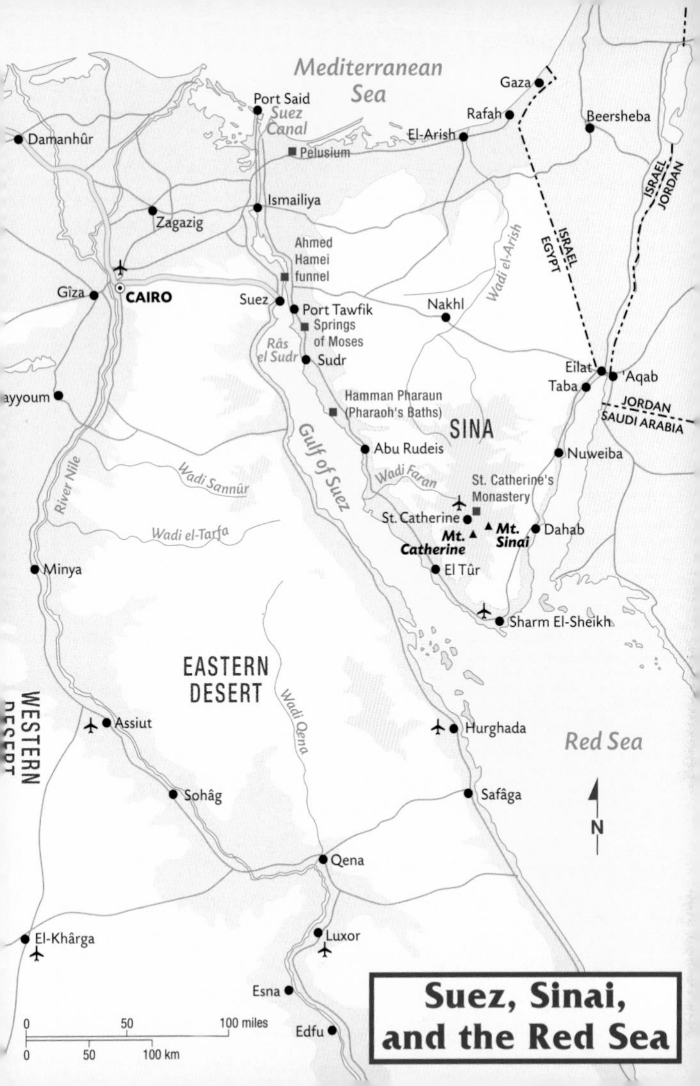

Suez, Sinai, and the Red Sea

Images of the Gods

Egypt was a large kingdom with many local and regional gods. Each major city was protected by a triad of gods; the major deities were all encompassing. Here is a basic introduction to the major deities.

Ra, or **Re:** Primal Creator Deity, controller of the universe, his symbols were the sun or obelisk. From the Fifth Dynasty, human rulers claimed from him a divine right to rule. Later Amun or Amon was identified with Ra and usually depicted in human form with a ram's head.

Isis: Goddess of fertility and motherhood. Normally represented in human form wearing a crown of cow horns.

Horus: Falcon-headed sun god and king of the Earth, who took human form in the ruling pharaoh.

Hathor: Goddess of love, laughter, beauty; patron of women and marriage. Depicted as a human with a cow's head, or as a star-studded cow. Consort of Horus.

Khephri: God of the sun and resurrection, who rolled the earth across the sky, depicted and personified by the scarab often worn as a lucky amulet in Egypt, even in modern times.

Anubis: God of the dead, depicted with the head of the jackal. He oversaw the mummification process and was also known as 'the divine embalmer.'

Nut: Sky goddess who swallowed the sun every evening and gave birth to it every morning.

Knum: ramheaded god of creation, protector of the source of the Nile.

Hapi/Hapy: god of the Nile, depicted with large stomach and pendulous breasts denoting health and fertility.

has long been the domain of the Bedouin, nomadic tribes who travel with their flocks of sheep and camels, moving from pasture to pasture and living in large family tents.

Favoured by the Ancient Egyptians as a source of turquoise, the Sinai was, until recently, famed for only one event – but certainly an important one. It was on one of its highest peaks, Mount Sinai (Gebel Musa), that Moses allegedly received the word of God, in the form of the Ten Commandments. These commandments form the structure for a number of the world's great religions.

In modern times the Sinai had become a backwater protected from the ravages of the modern world, and perhaps it would have remained one of the world's undiscovered spots if it hadn't been for one invention: Self Contained Underwater Breathing Apparatus (SCUBA). The waters around the coast are some of the clearest in the world and the depths are filled with amazingly diverse coral and many species of fish and other marine creatures.

In the 1950s and 1960s **Sharm El-Sheikh** on the southern tip of the Sinai became a divers' paradise and since then this small village has grown and spread north along several adjacent bays. Hundreds of hotels have sprung up along the sandy beaches, and these have been followed by restaurants, bars and shops, making today's Sharm El-Sheikh not just a diving destination but a true tourist resort. Sharm itself has little charm, but **Na'am Bay**, some 5 km (3 miles) further north, has a wonderful sandy beach, modern hotels and just about everything you could wish for in order to have a fun-filled holiday. Book ahead during the high season, as divers come from the world over.

In the 1980s, the Egyptian government had the sense to protect the precious waters of the south Sinai and created **Ras Mohammed National Park**, now home to over 1,000

The barren landscape of the Sinai fosters precious little vegetation, but this Acacia tree manages to thrive.

species of fish, marine animals and corals. Considered one of the premier diving sites in the world, it encompasses several different underwater environments in addition to coastal shallows where colourful fish thrive in the warm water. Divers can explore the deeps but you can also snorkel here, or take a glass-bottom boat or submarine tour to get a glimpse of this watery world. Ras Mohammed also protects the environment along the shoreline of the Sinai, including rare mangrove forests with abundant bird life.

Tourist development in the Sinai is mainly along the east coast where it meets the waters of the Gulf of Aqaba, though there can be many miles between resorts. Both **Dahab** and **Nuweiba** are growing but remain less developed than Sharm El-Sheikh. Holidaymakers come for the great diving, windsurfing and other watersports. At the very northern tip of the Sinai is **Taba**, with several large hotels, marking the Egyptian-Israeli border.

Mount Sinai and St. Catherine's Monastery

Mount Sinai has drawn pilgrims for generations and it was endowed with a Christian place of worship as early as AD 527, when Emperor Justinian built a small orthodox monastery in the lea of the mountain surrounded by sheer rock faces, in order to protect the Sinai passes against invasion. The church was built on what is thought to be the spot where Moses confronted the Burning Bush, but the Christian community had to confront far more mortal danger in the years following its foundation and its high and sturdy protective walls give it the look of a fortress rather than a place of worship.

The complex within the walls, still home to a community of Greek Orthodox priests, is centred around the **Church of St. Catherine**, built in 552 and dedicated to the saint when her remains were discovered nearby (on Mount St. Catherine) over 300 years later. The church houses some of the treasures of the monastery, which have been donated by wealthy benefactors throughout the past 1,500 years.

St. Catherine's has long been a very wealthy and influential monastery, founding schools in Greece and around the Orthodox world. The richly decorated iconostasis has highly regarded icons painted by Jeremias of Crete in 1612, but the 6th-century mosaics on the ceiling of the apse are the church's most impressive feature. St. Catherine's skull lies within her marble tomb, carved in the 18th century.

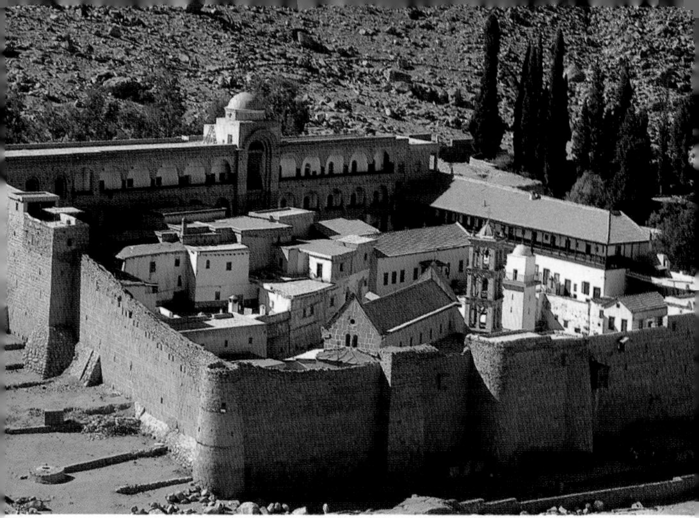

St. Catherine's Monastery is said to be built upon the spot where Moses encountered the fabled Burning Bush.

The smaller **Church of the Burning Bush** is situated within the complex, marking the spot where the bush is said to have grown. Many guides point out a verdant plant in the courtyard and insist it is a regeneration of the original.

Today you'll share your visit with hundreds of tourists, as the monastery is within easy reach of all the Sinai resorts, but not many venture up the slope to the top of Mount Sinai to visit the tiny chapel and take in the truly spectacular views of the surrounding mountains. It is an almost spiritual experience at sunrise when the sun's rays break over a silent world. The hike takes around two hours and you can travel the lower slopes by camel if you'd rather not walk the whole way. If you intend to start early take warm clothing – and don't forget your camera.

HIGHLIGHTS

The Egyptian Museum: Tahrir Square, Cairo; Tel. 2 574 2681. The world's greatest collection of ancient Egyptian artefacts. Open daily 9am–5pm.

The Pyramids of Giza and the Sphinx: Monumental tombs of pharaohs dating from around 2,600 BC. Open daily 8am–5pm.

Karnak Temple: Largest ancient temple complex in Egypt, centre of worship for Amun-Ra. Open daily 6am–5.30pm in winter, 6am–6.30pm in summer.

Luxor Temple: Temple of the New Year celebration to the god Amun. Open daily 9am–1pm, 4pm–9pm in winter; 5pm–10pm in summer.

Valley of the Kings: Underground tombs of the Theban pharaohs. Open daily 6am–5pm.

Denderah Temple: 60 km (43 miles) north of Luxor. Ptolemaic temple dedicated to the goddess Hathor. Open daily 8am–4pm.

Edfu Temple: 50 km (30 miles) south of Luxor. Temple to the god Horus. Open daily 8am–4pm.

Philae Temple: 12 km (6½ miles) south of Aswan. Temple to the goddess Isis, considered the most beautiful in Ancient Egypt. Open daily 8am–4pm.

Abu Simbel: Monumental temple of Ramses II. Open daily 8am–4pm.

Ras Mohammed National Park: Sharm El-Sheikh, Sinai; Some of the best diving in the world in this protected underwater and land-based National Park. Open daily 8am–4pm. Identification needed for entrance.

St. Catherine's Monastery: St. Catherine's, Sinai. Sixth-century monastery located in the shadow of Mount Sinai – said to be the place where Moses received the Ten Commandments. Open daily 9am–11.45am.

WHAT TO DO

ENTERTAINMENT

Sound and Light Shows: All the most impressive ancient sites in Egypt have a sound and light show, and it adds an extra theatrical dimension to your Egypt experience. Stirring music and dramatic soundtrack accompany the dance of lights over the monuments. At Giza the pyramids have a show nightly in English. At Luxor the show is held at Karnak temple (though Luxor temple is floodlit) where visitors spend half the show seated and the other half wandering among the obelisks and columns as the story unfolds. The Aswan sound and light show takes place at Philae Temple some 20 minutes away. Remember to take a warm layer of clothing if you intend to see a show during the winter months, as the evenings can be chilly.

For information on all sound and light shows, tel: (02) 386 3469; fax: (02) 385 2880; website <www.sound-light.egypt.com>.

Folkloric Events: The Bedouin of the Sinai have a fascinating lifestyle. Though many have now traded their wandering ways for permanent settlements, they still prefer to live in tents rather than houses and treasure their traditional social habits. Some families have opened up their homes to visitors and you can have an evening meal with them and discover more about their world.

In Upper Egypt, Nubian floorshows have a different atmosphere and flavour. They are performed in all the large hotels, and feature traditional music and dancing from this most ancient Egyptian culture.

Most large hotels will have a floorshow featuring music and dance, including a voluptuous belly-dancer, who will introduce the audience to the art of gyrating Egyptian-style. You'll probably be invited to join in as the evening progresses.

Clubs and Discos: Belly-dancing is not just a tourist show, it's also popular with Egyptians and you can take in a serious and perhaps more earthy show at several clubs around the capital. Discos are also popular – some of the most popular can be found at the major international hotels – and have a regular Egyptian clientele in addition to attracting visitors.

Casinos: There are more than a dozen casinos in Cairo, mostly in the major hotels, and they attract a number of serious "high rollers". Egyptian nationals are not allowed to gamble, so casinos are only open to foreign guests over the age of 21 (you will be asked for ID). Stakes are priced in US dollars and you can usually play blackjack, roulette, poker and baccarat. Slot machines are also available.

Opera: The Cairo Opera House opened in 1988 as a gift from the Japanese government. Performances are staged between October and May. Formal dress may be required.

Egyptian National Circus: The national circus started with the help of skilled Soviet practitioners in the 1960s, and it has a permanent base at Azouga in Cairo for most of the year. In summer the whole troupe moves to Alexandria to escape the heat and humidity of the capital.

SPORTS

Beaches and Watersports: You'll find wonderful fine sand beaches all along the Red Sea coast, the west coast of the Sinai Peninsula and its southern tip, and also along the Mediterranean coast. In general, the first two areas are more organised for foreign tourists; the Mediterranean caters to a much more domestic market. Sharm El Sheikh and Hurghada are the largest resorts, well-equipped with hotels and eateries, with a full range of facilities such as windsurfing, water-skiing, and water rides: Dahab and Nuweiba on the west coast of the Sinai are smaller, with a hardened diving or windsurfing crowd – great for a low-key vacation. Because daytime temperatures rarely drop below the 70s Farenheit (20s Centigrade), this area is a good year-round option for a fun-filled and a sun-filled vacation.

Snorkelling and Diving: Egypt is a great place for both diving and snorkelling – the southern tip of the Sinai Peninsula is one of the world's prime dive sites. Ras Mohammed National Park has over 1,500 species of fish and 150 types of coral along with an offshore vertical sea wall. These offer a variety of habitats and diving for all abilities. The reefs run all the way up the eastern coast of the Sinai Peninsula making Dahab and Naweiba good bases – though quieter then Sharm El Sheikh – for diving excursions. Hurghada sits across a small strait from Ras Mohammed National Park and the sea and coral life is excellent.

Dahab is a developing resort where you can enjoy great diving, windsurfing, and other watersports.

Hurghada is one of Egypt's most popular spots for diving. Here a group takes a break between exploring the depths.

If you wish to learn to dive in Egypt there is an excellent network of dive centres that offer training for beginners up to professionals. All centres are affiliated with one of the major certifying bodies. PADI (Professional Association of Diving Instructors) is the most common. The basic qualification, the Open Water certificate, takes five days to complete. On completion this will allow you to dive with an instructor to a depth of 18 metres (60 ft), which opens many dive sites in Egypt to you.

Many centres also offer an introductory session commonly known as the "Discover Scuba Programme". This involves a morning or afternoon of theory and swimming pool work, which will give you the chance to try out the basic techniques. Many large hotels offer this "taster" as a facility for their guests.

Emperor Divers is a long-established operation with offices at Hurghada, Na'am Bay and Nuweiba. Full details can be found at their website <www.emperordivers.com>.

If you don't want to dive then you can snorkel just offshore along the Red Sea and Sinai coasts to see excellent tropical marine life. If you don't have your own equipment it is easy to buy at the resort.

Other water-based activities include a glass-bottomed boat-ride or a trip under the water in the Aquascope submarine to see the excellent underwater environment. This is situated in the main harbour at Sharm El Sheikh, tel: 069 662252.

Fishing: All the resorts along the Red Sea coast, in the Sinai and along the Mediterranean have marinas where you will be able to rent boats for a morning or day's fishing. The fishing is excellent, and some companies will even set up a barbecue so that you can enjoy your catch the same day.

Safaris and Desert Adventures: Over 90 percent of Egypt's land is desert, making it only a matter of time before it became a tourist resource. With so many people trying to get away from it all, it is the perfect contrast to our urban existence. You can take safaris lasting from one to three days on camel, or by four-wheel-drive where all supplies are included, or simply head off on quad bikes for an afternoon of fun in the sand dunes. The Sinai region is best organised for these activities, though the Western Desert is developing. The Hurghada Adventures Club offers professional and multilingual fully insured quad safaris; contact them at Friendship Village, tel: 010 156 7571; website <www.geocities.com/hurghada_adventures>.

Camel and Horseback-riding: Motor vehicles are only recent arrivals in Egypt and traditional forms of transport are still popular with Egyptians making great holiday activities.

Camel rides and treks can be taken around the pyramids, at Luxor and Aswan, at every resort in the Sinai and on the Red Sea coast. Horseback-riding is also well organised in the Sinai and the Red Sea, although less so along the Nile Valley.

Other Sports: If you feel the need to work up a sweat while you are in Cairo then you can become a temporary member of the Gazira Sports Club – once the domain of the upper classes. Situated on Zamelek Island, the club features an amazing array of facilities including tennis courts, squash courts, handball courts and several swimming pools. The Oberoi Mena House Hotel operates an 18-hole golf club in the shadow of the pyramids at Giza, and you don't need to be a guest to enjoy the facilities.

SHOPPING

There's something for all budgets in Egypt. The skills of carvers, weavers and painters have been passed down through the generations and you can really have fun for hours browsing at the wares. However, the Egyptians are tenacious shopkeepers and you will need a will of steel and a sense of humour to shrug off their sales pitch.

Where to Shop

Bazaars: Khan El Khalili in Cairo is one of the oldest and most renowned bazaars in the Islamic world, and it is a veritable treasure-trove of shopping opportunities. The labyrinth of narrow alleys constitutes several different "quarters", each specialising in a particular skill or merchandise. One of the most fascinating is the tent-making area, where large ceremonial marquis-style tents are fashioned by hand from brightly dyed Egyptian cotton. Stroll around and mingle with Egyptians doing their own shopping – Khan El Khalili is not just a tourist bazaar – to find handicrafts and artefacts from around the country.

Luxor has a smaller but no less atmospheric bazaar, and Aswan has a great shopping street running one block parallel to the river.

Archaeological Sites: Mini-tourist markets have sprung up around most of the major archaeological sites, and they all sell much the same items, but prices are likely to be higher than at the larger bazaars.

When shopping, be aware that quality does vary greatly and some bargains may not be what they appear – inferior stone painted to look like marble or alabaster is a favourite ploy around the sites in Upper Egypt. Always study any item carefully before purchase.

You'll find prices begin to drop at the end of the day, after the tour groups leave, especially out of season.

Shopping Tips

If you take a guide or interpreter with you, it is customary for them to receive a percentage on every purchase you make.

At reputable vendors you will be able to arrange for the shipping of items that are too large to carry or too fragile to check on the return flight home.

There's no shortage of souvenirs in Aswan.

Haggling

Few prices are fixed in Egypt and thus a protracted discussion will begin, the purpose of which is to agree a price that satisfies both buyer and seller – in other words, "haggling."

Remember that negotiations should be undertaken with good humour; this is not a battle, it's more a form of verbal gymnastics meant to achieve a win-win situation. Cups of tea or coffee are traditionally offered to oil the wheels of the deal – although today you may be offered the ubiquitous cola instead – and if you are serious about buying, don't turn this down as it's a symbolic stepping-stone marking you apart from the mere browser. The starting price is always high. Don't accept it but don't insult the vendor with a ludicrously low counter-offer. You'll probably end up with a price that's around 50–70 percent of this initial price so if the goods are genuinely more expensive than you want to pay, better to walk away now with a handshake and a firm "no thank you". If you want to proceed, make your lower offer but have a higher final price in mind; you'll reach it gradually while your host takes great pains to explain how good the quality of his product is as against those of his neighbours. One good tip is to agree on a strategy with any companions beforehand – feigned nonchalance by your friend can work in your favour.

And at the end of the day have fun; once the deal is sealed, you'll definitely come home having bought something exciting and individual.

What to Buy

Alabaster and Marble: Carving skills have been passed down through the centuries, particularly in villages near the Valley of the Kings and around the marble quarries at Aswan. You can find myriad copies of ancient pieces – from obelisks to pyramids – and incredibly kitsch and tacky copies of Ancient Egyptian artefacts such as Tutankhamun's mask, but also wonderful hand-carved vases, bowls and urns. Small items, such as scarab beetles – considered a lucky amulet in Egypt – are sold in shops, but also by young children and street hawkers around the archaeological sites.

Copper and Brass: These metals have long been used for practical items such as water carriers, samovars or cooking pots and they make excellent souvenirs. Older pieces have the patina of age, whereas new pieces – usually made on-site – are bright and shiny. Trays can be found in all sizes and those with a wooden stand make wonderful portable tables for the home.

Cotton and Woollen Goods: Egypt is famed for its fine cotton. The thousands of hectares under cultivation in the Nile Delta are one of the country's most lucrative export earners. For the domestic market you'll find practical items such as the *gellabiya* – the long shirt-like garment – and T-shirts, normally featuring images of camels and pyramids. For men, *gellabiyas* are usually plain, perhaps with a little collar detail, but for women you can find brightly decorated versions, often bedecked with sequins. You'll also find skimpy belly-dancing outfits if you want to be daring.

Other natural fibres are made into beautiful scarves, shawls and blankets – often used as wraps by Egyptians to keep the winter chills at bay and woven with rich patterns in earth tones or deep reds. Sheep wool is the most common and therefore the cheapest, followed by camel hair, which is exceptionally soft. Most expensive are silk or silk-blended items.

Jewellery: It's not surprising, given the amount of gold thought to have been buried in Egyptian tombs – like the riches found in Tutankhamun's in the 1920s – that gold and jewellery is a good buy in modern Egypt. Precious metals are sold by weight, with very little added to the price for workmanship. Precious stones and semi-precious stones including topaz, lapis lazuli and aquamarine, can be bought loose or set in rings, necklaces, bracelets or brooches. Hieroglyphic *cartouches* are also popular souvenirs – a jeweller can have your name made up into a *cartouche* of Egyptian script in just a couple of days.

Woodwork: Islam frowns on the use of precious metals in its religious buildings, so artisans working more basic raw materials have always been highly regarded in the Arab world. Egypt – particularly Cairo – is famous for its wood carvers, who still produce beautiful hand-worked pieces in small workshops in the old part of the city. From the smallest box to large coffee tables, the intricate detail is exquisite. The finest and most authentic work is *mashrabiya*, the lattice screens that covered Ottoman windows allowing women to watch the world go by without being seen. This is now reproduced in small scale for picture frames or as room screens, which make an excellent statement in a modern living room. Look also for boxed chess and backgammon sets made from wood inlaid with pieces fashioned from mother of pearl or ivory. Don't worry about the risk to endangered animal species – most Egyptian ivory is camel or donkey bone, not elephant tusk.

Papyrus: The leaves of the papyrus were dried and used by Ancient Egyptians as a form of paper. The art of papyrus-making was lost in Egypt until the 1970s when it was reintroduced using native plants. Today, it is possible to buy cheap papyrus printed with gaudy Egyptian scenes in almost every souvenir shop in the country, but some of the most authentic are sold at The Pharaonic Village in Cairo where the papyrus is grown, processed and hand-painted on site.

Perfume: The élite of Ancient Egypt enjoyed a leisurely life, surrounding themselves with incense, unguents and perfumes made from petals and oils. Perfumes are still popular today and you will see the perfume blender at the bazaar surrounded by hundreds of glass bottles containing the numerous oils that he combines to make a single scent. Blenders will copy your favourite Western perfume, or will suggest a blend to suit your skin type, and you can buy an ornate glass perfume bottle in which to put it. If you don't want the perfume, the bottles are on sale in many souvenir shops and make pretty decorative pieces.

Spices: The long north and east trade routes that came together in Egypt for centuries made it an international marketplace for many spices; you can still find interesting flavourings on sale, along with the dried hibiscus flowers used to make sweet tea.

THINGS TO DO WITH CHILDREN

Long hot days touring temples, tombs and museums are not going to be at the top of most children's lists of great things to do on holiday, but there are lots of ways to make their trip fun.

- When visiting the pyramids, let kids enjoy a camel or horse ride out across the site. You'll be able to hire camels and horses at Luxor and Aswan and at numerous resorts along the Red Sea and in the Sinai.
- Don't miss the mummy room at the Cairo museum. Kids will love the slightly gory-looking pharaohs and will be fascinated by the process of mummification – though it's not for the faint-hearted.
- Take a *felucca* (a narrow lateen-rigged boat) ride on the Nile – it's fun being out on the water for children and adults alike.
- Visit the Pharaonic Village and let children see Ancient Egyptian daily life rather than just imagining it.
- Ride in a horse-drawn carriage along the corniche next to the Nile at Luxor or Aswan – this high vantage point gives children a great view of what's happening.
- Book a hotel with a pool, so that after a day sightseeing, you can have a relaxing swim and some childish fun. For children too young to dive or snorkel, take glass-bottom boat rides or visit the Aquascope submarine to get an excellent view of the marine life.

Calendar of Events

Many of Egypt's primary holidays are based on the Muslim calendar, which is calculated on the changing lunar cycle. Please check with the Egyptian Tourist Authority (see page 125) *for exact festival dates in the year that you are travelling.*

7 January: Coptic Christmas with presents and partying for the Christian community.

Coptic Good Friday: 2003 – 25 April; 2004 – 9 April; 2005 – 29 April; 2006 – 21 April; 2007 – 6 April; 2008 – 25 April.

Coptic Easter

Shäm En Nessim: the National Spring Festival, held the first Monday after Coptic Easter, when the whole population comes out to celebrate.

Ramadan Bairam is a month long celebration when Muslims fast during the hours of daylight. There are nightly *iftah* (special Ramadan dishes) at sunset, with families gathering to celebrate. Also gifts and celebrations on *Eid El-Fitr*, the last three days of the festival. Approximate dates: 2002 – 6 November; 2003 – 27 October; 2004 – 15 October; 2005 – 9 October; 2006 – 24 September; 2007 – 13 September; 2008 – 2 September.

Mulid En Nabi is another major holiday – it celebrates the Prophet's Birthday.

Qurban Bairam (Eid El-Adha) is a time when many Muslims travel to Mecca to commemorate the slaying of Abraham. Just as in the Bible, when a ram was substituted for Abraham, lambs are slaughtered, cooked, and shared by families or among local neighbourhoods.

The Cairo Film Festival is held every December with screenings of major international films taking place at various hotels all across Cairo.

EATING OUT

The staples of Egyptian cuisine have changed little since the time of the pharaohs. Rice, wheat and vegetables are grown along the Nile valley and in its fertile delta; meat comes from the herds of sheep and goats, or the ducks and geese and pigeons kept by almost every household. These are supplemented by fresh fish from the Red and Mediterranean seas, as well as from the Nile River itself.

During the last millennium, as Egypt came under foreign domination, other culinary influences melded with these domestic ingredients, and both Ottoman and British dishes have found their way onto most Egyptian menus.

Egypt has developed an exceptionally good range of international restaurants to cater to its growing number of visitors. These are often based in large hotels in the main tourist towns and the capital: some hotels have five or six eateries, each specialising in a different type of cuisine. Foreign chefs preside over the kitchens to ensure that dishes feature authentic ingredients and cooking methods.

When to Eat

Most hotels will serve a Continental-style breakfast, but larger luxury-class hotels will lay on a superb buffet with cereals, fruit, cold cooked meats, and hot dishes.

If you want to eat as the Egyptians do, then lunch should be the main meal of the day, eaten from 1–3pm. Dinner in Egyptian homes is a smaller meal eaten as late as 10pm; however, the tourist industry caters to visitors' eating habits and there is no shortage of eateries serving main meals in the evenings from around 6pm to 11pm or midnight.

During the month of Ramadan, when Muslims fast during the hours of daylight, special arrangements are made for both the meal to break the fast *(iftah)* and the meal to commence the fast *(sohour)* with particular foods prepared for each. During Ramadan, most international hotels continue to open restaurants as normal for foreign guests, but if you are travelling around the country, most independent restaurants will not serve food during the day, so you'll need to make contingency plans for lunch and an early dinner.

EGYPTIAN CUISINE

When tourism began to grow in Egypt and the number of restaurants began to increase rapidly, Egyptian cuisine took a back seat to international fare. Although many people enjoy being able to have a little taste of home, hoteliers are thankfully beginning to have confidence in native dishes and there are a number of excellent restaurants serving Egyptian food. Do make time to try some of the local dishes, which you'll discover are both exquisite and nutritious.

Appetisers

Many Egyptians begin a meal with a shared plate of *mezzeh*, small portions of several dishes. The most popular are local cheeses, salads, stuffed vine leaves, *kofta* (fried meatballs with spices and coriander), *makhallal* (pickled vegetables) – sometimes also served as an accompaniment to main dishes – *tabouleh* (crushed bulgar wheat mixed with parsley, mint, finely chopped tomatoes and onions), tahini (sesame seed purée), *leban zabada* (yoghurt), and *baba ganoug* (tahini with puréed aubergine flesh, garlic and lemon juice). These last three are scooped up with fresh warm pitta (unleavened bread) cooked in a wood-fired oven.

Soups are another popular choice. *Molokhia* is a savoury broth of greens cooked with garlic, pepper and coriander – you may also find an extra ingredient such as rice or chicken. Lentil soup can be found all across Egypt and fish soup is served along the coastline. One traditional dish will be served at any meal and is a favourite to break the Ramadan fast; *ful*, a thick spicy bean stew flavoured with tomatoes. It is commonly served with oil and fresh lime juice and accompanied by *taamia*, deep-fried bean paste flavoured with vegetables, spices and parsley.

Main Dishes

Meat: Though meat has always been seen as a luxury ingredient in the diet of ordinary Egyptians, they have developed some delicious ways of serving it. Most common is lamb or goat, and on feast days whole animals are cooked and served in neighbourhood parties – a well-developed facet of Arab hospitality and charity. Barbecueing is the most popular cooking method, over an open charcoal grill or a covered wood-fired oven. Lamb and goat is often marinated in fresh herbs and spices that enhance the meaty flavour.

Kebabs are chunks of meat threaded on to a skewer; try *kofta* – minced lamb shaped around the skewer, or *shwarma* – lamb roasted on a vertical spit, thinly sliced and served with salad and pitta bread.

Grilled or barbecued chicken is also found on

Enjoy views of the Cairo Tower during dinner on a floating restaurant.

every menu – it arrives hot and meltingly tender. Less common is duck or goose, but it is delicious when you can find it.

Pigeons *(hamam)* are kept by many Egyptians – look for whitewashed dovecotes on house roofs as you travel around – and quail is popular in season. Both birds are generally stuffed before being cooked, and are then served on a bed of rice.

Fish: You'll be spoilt for choice when it comes to seafood, though prices are higher than for meat dishes. From the Mediterranean and Red seas, you'll find sea bream, red and grey mullet, and sea bass.

Alexandrian shrimp – large and succulent – are a speciality of the area, though numbers are falling, and you'll find spiny lobster from the Red Sea along with squid and cuttlefish. The Nile provides little commercial fishing, though freshwater tilapia from Lake Nasser is excellent.

Again the grill features quite prominently in cooking. Most whole fish are simply grilled unadorned and served with fresh lemon wedges. A delicacy that is now quite rare is *betarek*, dried salted cod roe served on bread soaked in olive oil; it is said that the Ancient Egyptians enjoyed it for its aphrodisiac powers.

Accompaniments

Rice is the most common dish to be served with main courses, though you can have potato chips (French fries). As most food in Egypt is served warm rather than hot (hot food is said to be bad for the digestion), those expecting crisp fries will no doubt be disappointed. Seasonal salads are available, including delicious plates of sliced beetroot or cucumber.

Desserts

Fresh fruits abound along the Nile Valley and in the Delta, growing in the fertile soil, and these make an excellent fresh dessert. Depending on the season, you'll be presented with bananas, oranges, figs, melons or guavas. Dates are also readily available and are delicious when fresh – totally different to the texture of dried dates. You'll see both varieties at the markets; the dried varieties are popular with Egyptians, many of whom spend long days in the fields; they provide slow-release energy and make a good option for carrying with you on your own archaeological explorations should you become jaded or ravenous.

If you are looking for something a little more substantial to finish your meal, you have a number of delicious options. Try a native Egyptian dish called *om-ali* (rice baked with milk, raisins and nuts), or treat yourself to one of the decadent desserts introduced during the years of Ottoman rule. *Baklava* (layers of butter-soaked flaky pastry interspersed with nuts and honey) is the most famous and is succulent and incredibly sweet. *Atayeef* is a delicious deep-fried sweet-filled pastry (sometimes also filled with cheese).

INTERNATIONAL CUISINE

You'll be able to find a whole range of international cuisine in Cairo and the tourist areas. Most major hotels have a range of eateries and standards are high – though the buffets can be a little bland – with some of the most renowned restaurants in Egypt found in hotels rather than private establishments. Look for restaurants that employ foreign chefs as a sign of commitment to authenticity. You'll be able to choose from Italian, French and Japanese cuisine, or head to the British pub or American diner if you want casual style.

Along the Red Sea and Sinai coasts, a growing destination with package tourists from Europe, you'll find a plethora of pizza parlours, bierkellers and Chinese restaurants. Many Egyptian restaurants now offer the familiar 'burger' in addition to other grilled meats.

DRINKS

Although Egypt is a Muslim country and most of its population does not drink alcohol, it does not prohibit its nationals or its foreign visitors from imbibing, and in fact has a thriving wine industry of its own. The soil of the Nile Delta is highly suitable for vine cultivation and you'll find quite palatable domestic labels in restaurants across the country. More expensive foreign wines can be found in the international hotels and finer restaurants but they carry a high mark-up.

Omar Khayyam and Kasr Gianaclis are soft and fairly dry reds; Pharaon reds are less sophisticated. White wines – Nefertiti, Cleopatra and Gianaclis Villages – are better than the reds but may not be served as cool as they should be. Rubis d'Egypte is a refreshing rosé that is excellent drunk on its own or with food.

If you want to try something a little stronger ask for *zibib*, an aniseed-flavoured spirit like Greek *ouzo* or French *pastis*, which is made from distilling grape skins; or request a strong and slightly sweeter date brandy.

Beers are imported, as is a comprehensive range of international spirits such as gin, whisky and cognac.

Tea *(shay)* is ubiquitous in Egypt. Served at all times of the day, offered at bazaars when you shop, and drunk by Egyptian men playing backgammon at cafés, it is hot and refreshing, served weak and without milk in little glasses. Ask for mint tea for a fresh sprig to be added to your cup.

The Ottoman Turks brought their own distinctive strong coffee with them after they took control, and it remains a favourite with Egyptians who enjoy it *ziyada* – with lots of sugar. If you find this too sweet for your palate try *mazbut* – medium – or *saadeh* – with no sugar. You could even try it with a slight pinch of salt to add to the already bitter coffee taste. Ask for it to come *arridah* and see what you think.

Tap water is off limits but there is a safe domestic bottled water sold all across Egypt. Another refreshing drink is made from dried hibiscus petals. Called *karkadeh*, it can be served chilled – very cooling in the summer – or hot as a tea. Said to aid digestion, it is often served at the start of the meal, especially during Ramadan.

Here are some useful words to help you order

bread	**esh**	dates	**balah**
butter	**zibda**	fish	**samek**
chicken	**fiakh**	meat	**fakha**
chickpeas	**hommos**	potatoes	**lahm**
coffee	**ahwa**	rice	**batatis**
soup	**shorba**	sugar	**sokkar**
wine	**nibit**	boiled	**maslook**
fried	**makli**	grilled	**mashwi**

A trip to Cairo would be incomplete if you didn't sample a traditional Egyptian meal.

HANDY TRAVEL TIPS

An A–Z Summary of Practical Information

A

ACCOMMODATION

Egypt has some excellent hotels in the higher star brackets but less choice in the lower price ranges. Many hotels in the three- to five-star range are contracted to tour group companies, so accommodation can be difficult to find at peak times: December–April in Cairo and along the Nile; June to August for Alexandria and the coastal areas.

Hotels also have expensive rack rates (rooms booked on spec – coming in off the street), meaning independent travellers are at a disadvantage. If possible, pre-book your accommodation through a travel agent before you leave for Egypt. A specialist agent will be able to confirm accommodation for custom-made complicated itineraries, or suggest a reputable company from whom you can buy a pre-set package. If you travel independently, do have confirmation of your bookings to avoid problems at check-in. Prices are normally quoted in US dollars and in three- to five-star hotels you will be able to pay in foreign currency or by credit card.

AIRPORTS

The main airport of entry into Egypt is Cairo – 20 km (12 miles) northwest of the downtown area. There are two terminals; Terminal One handles all Egypt Air and other Egyptian airline flights, Middle Eastern and Eastern European Airline services; Terminal Two for all American and Western European airlines. You'll need to have some small notes on arrival to tip the porters. There are taxi, bus and Misr Travel Care coaches from the airport. If your plane departs during the day (8am– 10pm), allow 2 hours to get from central Cairo to the airport as traffic is always congested along the airport road.

There are also airports at Alexandria, Aswan, Hurghada, Luxor and Sharm El-Sheikh. These local airports handle domestic flights from Cairo and many international charter flights from Western Europe. Both airport terminals at Cairo have bank and visa facilities but queues can be long at peak times. If possible, obtain visas and a limited amount of Egyptian currency before you travel.

B

BICYCLE RENTAL

Cycling along the corniches at Aswan and Luxor is a relaxing way of getting to know the towns. Taking a bike across the Nile from Luxor to the Valley of the Kings is also a great way to appreciate the landscape of the Nile Valley.

Bicycles can be rented very cheaply, 20LE for a day (look for painted signs offering rental), but do examine them before you set out to make sure they are working effectively. There is no safety equipment available.

BUDGETING FOR YOUR TRIP

Air fare: London–Cairo from £250, New York–Cairo $400.

Charter Air fare: London–Luxor/London–Sharm El Sheik £149–225

Air fare: Cairo–Luxor $90

Air fare: Aswan–Abu Simbel $80.

Room per night in moderate hotel: $80–120.

Dinner per person in moderate restaurant: 70–100LE.

Entrance fee to the Giza Pyramids: 40LE.

Sound and Light Show: 33LE.

Entrance fee to Luxor Temple: 20LE

Camel ride at the pyramids: from 10LE depending on length.

Taxi fare: Cairo–Airport: 55LE.

Daily taxi rental: from 500LE.

Windsurf Rental: 180LE per day/50LE per hour.

Horseback-riding: 50LE/hour.

C

CAMPING

There are camping facilities along the Nile valley, at the Oases and the Mediterranean, Red Sea and Sinai coasts. Details can be obtained from the Egyptian Tourist Board.

CAR RENTAL

Car rental in Egypt is expensive and the driving is difficult *(see DRIVING)*. Cairo's road system and the habits of the drivers make it almost impossible to navigate, and the plentiful and cheap taxis are a better bet.

Following the terrorist attacks in the late 1990s, independent travel along the Nile Valley and across to the Red Sea is impossible for foreigners. A system of convoys has been devised to give military protection to foreign travellers whether on guided tours or going it alone. Travellers must work within the convoy timetable and must report to the local police station to liaise with them.

One area that is still best seen by rental car is the Sinai; roads are generally quiet and in good condition, and exploring the area offers wonderful desert landscapes and the opportunity to learn something about the Bedouin lifestyle.

Car rental is available from Cairo Airport or from major hotels in the capital. In the Red Sea and Sinai resorts car rental companies have offices along the main streets. Be aware that vehicles may not be new and may have had previous damage, so check them thoroughly before driving away.

Most short-term contracts will be "limited kilometres" only, so try to estimate how many kilometres you will drive in order to arrive at an overall price.

Always check the small print on contracts and find out who is responsible for damage should an accident occur. Many companies have high damage excesses. The international companies work under franchise in Egypt and it may offer more peace of mind to pre-book through them before you travel so that you can discuss and agree on the clauses of the rental's small print.

Drivers must be over 21 years of age and have a full national driving licence. An international driving licence would be helpful. It is better to pay with a credit card, as you will need to pay a large cash deposit if not.

Avis: Cairo International Airport, tel: (02) 2265 2429; Sharm El-Sheikh, tel: (062) 602 400; Hurghada, tel: 65 447 400; website <www.avis.com>.

Hertz: Cairo International Airport, tel: (02) 2652430; Sharm El-Sheikh, tel: (069) 600 459; Hurghada, tel: (065) 442 884; website <www.hertz.com>.

Budget: Cairo International Airport, tel: (02) 265 2395; Sharm El-Sheikh, tel: (062) 601 610; Hurghada, tel: (065) 411 122; website <www.budget.com>.

CLIMATE

October and November are the best months to visit Egypt. The summer heat has dissipated and the winter chills have not yet set in. Summers can be stifling, especially in Upper Egypt, with temperatures climbing well over 100°F (37°C). Most hotels, tour buses and Nile cruise ships have air-conditioning, but sightseeing really has to be restricted to early and late in the day to avoid the worst of the sun. It is also hot in the Sinai and along the Red Sea coast.

		J	F	M	A	M	J	J	A	S	O	N	D
Cairo	°C	14	15	18	21	23	27	29	28	26	24	20	15
	°F	57	59	64	70	76	81	84	82	79	75	68	59
Alexandria													
	°C	14	15	16	19	22	24	26	27	25	23	20	16
	°F	57	59	61	66	72	75	79	81	77	76	68	61

Egypt

Winter is warm in Upper Egypt, with daytime temperatures still rising to the mid to high 70s Farenheit (mid 20s Centigrade). Evenings can be chilly, especially in the Sinai where night frost is not unknown.

Cairo and the north have temperatures in the high 60s and low 70s Farenheit (low 20s Centigrade) in winter. Again evenings can feel chilly. Rain is almost unknown in Egypt – only Alexandria and the Mediterranean coast see a measurable amount. The Red Sea and Sinai coastlines benefit from sea breezes in summer, which can develop into quite strong winds in winter.

CLOTHING

If you are travelling in summer you'll need only light clothing wherever you go in Egypt. Cotton and silk are ideal. In winter, although it is still warm during the day, you'll need to take extra layers for the evenings. Always carry sunglasses (the sandstone monuments along the Nile can be surprisingly bright in the sunshine) and a hat for shade.

If you are travelling in the mountains in the Sinai – especially up Mount Sinai – take a warm layer. You may find that the temperature differences between sunshine and shade can make you feel chilly. Warm clothing is necessary after dark in the desert at all times of the year.

Shoes should be flat and comfortable for sightseeing in the city or at the temple sites. They should be sturdy in order to take the uneven surfaces, dust and hills that you may encounter. Heels should be reserved for dinner only.

In large 5-star hotels and on certain Nile cruise vessels you may be asked to dress smart-casual – this may include jacket and tie for the men. Cairenes enjoy dressing up to attend fine restaurants, but otherwise Egypt is a casual destination. Remember that this is an Islamic country and modest dress is most sensible for both men and women – nothing too short or revealing is the best bet for touring and sightseeing.

Always remove shoes when visiting mosques (or use the covers provided). Shorts are not allowed when you visit mosques or churches, so lightweight trousers for both sexes make the most sensible choice for a day of varied sightseeing.

COMPLAINTS

In the first instance you should take up your grievance with the management of the organisation concerned. If you still feel unhappy contact the Tourist Police or the local police at your location *(see POLICE)*. They are usually cooperative.

Many tourist complaints stem from overcharging in cafés and bars. In a country where there are few set prices, it is always advisable to ask before you order to avoid the feeling of being "fleeced".

CRIME AND SAFETY

Egypt is, by and large, a very law-abiding country with very few serious crimes committed against visitors. The terrorist attacks against tourists in the Nile valley in the 1990s were politically motivated and do not indicate a general dislike and targeting of visitors. The Egyptian government now closely controls tourist travel along the Nile Valley in Upper Egypt and from the Nile Valley to the Red Sea.

Petty crime is rising however, especially in the more popular tourist areas and crowded areas such as the markets. To avoid becoming a victim of crime, take the following precautions:

- Never carry large amounts of cash.
- Leave all valuables in the hotel safe.
- Guard bags and pockets, especially in crowded areas.
- Always walk in well-lit streets at night.
- Do not leave valuables on the beach when you swim.
- It is always useful to have copies of important paperwork

such as ticket numbers, passport number, and travellers' cheque numbers just in case you do find yourself a victim.

CUSTOMS AND ENTRY REQUIREMENTS

Visas: All visitors to Egypt need a transit visa for stays of up to seven days or a tourist visa for stays not exceeding one month (extendable for up to six months). These are supplied from the Egyptian embassy in your home country or at the airport on arrival at a cost of $15/£11 – foreign currency only. These allow you to travel in all areas of Egypt.

If you are travelling from Israel, make sure that you get a full visa as there is also a 'Sinai only' visa which will not allow travel onto mainland Egypt. Because of ongoing problems within Israel, do enquire about the current travel situation between the two countries before you depart.

All visitors must register with the Interior Ministry in Tahrir Square, Cairo within seven days of arrival. If you are travelling with a group this should be done for you, and most large hotels will take care of it for you. Make enquiries when you check in. Those wanting to extend their stay beyond one month will need to have proof of an Aids test.

Customs Limits: If you intend to travel with expensive camera, video or computer equipment, it would be wise to declare it on entry. Details will be noted and you will then be asked to produce it on your departure to prove you have not sold it during your stay.

Prohibited items are drugs, firearms, and cotton.

All visitors may bring the following items into Egypt duty-free:

- 200 cigarettes or 25 cigars or 200g of tobacco.
- 2 litres of alcohol.
- A reasonable amount of perfume.
- Gifts to the value of 500LE.

Currency restrictions: No more than 1,000LE can be imported or exported. There are no limits on the amounts of foreign currency imported or exported but it must be declared on entry. The currency declaration form should be stamped by customs on entry, and kept, with all currency exchange receipts, in the event it may be examined on your departure.

D

DRIVING

As a result of the terrorist attacks around Luxor in Upper Egypt in the late 1990s, security systems have been put in place to minimise the risk to tourists. All tourist travel is controlled and a system of convoys with military guards operates in Upper Egypt. If you book a tour with a company the arrangements will all be taken care of, but if you want to travel independently (by rental car or taxi) you must report to the police where you will be told the time of the convoys. You will have to report to travel with a convoy – you will not be able to travel as you want, or stop along the convoy route.

The convoy system covers the following routes along the Nile Valley in Upper Egypt: from Luxor north (including Denderah and Abydos temples); from Aswan to Luxor and vice versa; Luxor to Hurghada and vice versa; and west of Luxor into the desert.

Road conditions: Road conditions are improving, with good routes north from Cairo to Alexandria, and throughout the Sinai. The main Nile Valley route on the east bank is undergoing repair and improvement but its condition still varies from good to appalling and care should be taken at all times. You'll find very slow and extremely fast traffic along your path. Most Egyptian drivers don't seem to obey any rules of the road so be aware. Overtaking is done in the face of oncoming traffic, and cars pull on and off the highway without indication. Numerous small buses weave in and out of traffic lanes, stopping frequently to pick up passengers. Vehicles, which in many countries would be unfit for the road, operate without restraint. Animals graze at the roadsides, wandering across the highways whenever they choose.

Rules and Regulations: In theory Egyptians drive on the left and pass on the right, though in practise no one seems to obey any rules of the road. Speed limits should be 100km/hr (62 mph) on dual highways and 90km/hr (56 mph) on other roads unless otherwise posted.

Fuel costs: Fuel is inexpensive and sold by the litre. Most modern gas pumps give price and quantity in Roman rather than Arabic numerals so that you can see how much you are buying and at what price.

Parking: Parking is difficult in Cairo. Most large hotels have a garage but may charge clients for its use.

If you need help: There are no breakdown services in Egypt but if you suffer a breakdown or accident there is a Red Crescent service that operates a network of small centres throughout the country. Ask for the telephone number of the nearest centre when you rent the vehicle.

For further information on driving laws and assistance, contact the Automobile Club of Egypt, 10 Sharia Kasr El Nil, Cairo, tel: (2) 574 3355.

Road signs: Road signs are rare, and distance signs should not necessarily be believed.

E

ELECTRICITY

Most of Egypt operates on the 220-volt, 50-cycle electric current, though the Alexandria region has the 110-volt 50-cycle system. Plugs are of the European two-pin variety. The electricity supply is prone to interruptions and variations in current, so be prepared for the occasional blackout. You will always find a candle and matches in hotel rooms for just such an eventuality.

EMBASSIES AND CONSULATES

Australia
Cairo Plaza
World Trade Centre, 11th floor
11111 Corniche El-Nil
Bulaq, Cairo
Tel: (2) 575 0444
Fax: (2) 578 1638
<www.dfat.gov.au/missions>

Canada
5 El Saraya El Kobre Square.
Arab International Bank Building
Garden City, Cairo.
Postal address: P.O. Box 1667.
Tel: (2) 794 3110
Fax: (2) 796 3548

Republic of Ireland
3 Abu El Fida Street, 7th floor
Zamalek, Cairo
Postal address: P.O. Box 2681
Tel: (2) 340 8264
Fax: (2) 341 2863
Email: irishemb@rite.com

South Africa
The nearest diplomatic office is in Athens, Greece.
60, Kifissias Avenue
151 25 Maroussi
Athens, Greece.
Tel: (30) 1 680 6645
Fax: (30) 1 680 6640

United Kingdom
7 Ahmed Ragheb Street,
Garden City, Cairo.
Tel: (2) 794 0850–8
Fax: (2) 794 0859/3065
<www.britishembassy.org.eg>

USA
5 Latin America Street,
Garden City, Cairo.
Tel: (2) 797 3300
Fax: (2) 797 3200
<www.usembassy.egnet.net>

New Zealand nationals should contact the United Kingdom Embassy for diplomatic aid.

EMERGENCY TELEPHONE NUMBERS

(See Crime and Safety)

Police **122**	Ambulance **123**
Cairo Tourist Police **126**	Fire **125**

G

GAY AND LESBIAN TRAVELLERS

Egypt is an Islamic country and has conservative values. Close physical contact between both heterosexual couples and same-sex couples is frowned upon and therefore there is no openly gay scene, though the major coastal resorts do have a more relaxed attitude – with more visitors from abroad and more of a night scene.

GETTING THERE

Egypt Air website <www.egyptair.com.eg> is the national carrier for Egypt and it operates a network of international services to London, Manchester, New York, Los Angeles, Cape Town, Johannesburg and Sydney. They also operate services to and from the following international hub airports in Europe: Amsterdam, Frankfurt, Geneva, Milan, Paris and Rome. For connection to Australia and New Zealand, Egypt Air operates a service to Singapore.

The following European airlines also fly to Cairo: British Airways (website <www.britishairways.com>), KLM (website <www.klm.com>), Lufthansa (website <www.lufthansa.com>), Air France (website <www.airfrance.com>) and Iberia (website <www.iberia.com>).

The following airlines can provide routings from North America to Cairo via a European hub: British Airways, KLM, Swiss Air, Air France, Alitalia (website <www.alitalia.com>) and Iberia.

Connections to Europe from North America for onward journey to Cairo can be made with Northwest Airlines (website <www.nwa.com>), Air Canada (website <www.aircanada.ca>), Continental Airlines (website <www.continental.com>), Delta Airlines (website <www. delta.com>), American Airlines (website <www.aa.com>) and Virgin Atlantic (website <www.virgin-atlantic.com>).

From Australia and New Zealand you can reach Europe for onward flights to Cairo with Singapore Airlines (website <www.singaporeair.com>), Thai Airways (website <www.thaiair.com>), Qantas (website <www.qantas.com>) and Air New Zealand (website <www.airnewzealand.co.nz>).

Visit an experienced travel agent in North America who can advise on the myriad group-inclusive tours or customised options available if you want a pre-booked itinerary for your trip.

Numerous European companies offer package holidays to Cairo and the Nile Valley, the Sinai and the Red Sea. The major providers are Kuoni (website <www.kuoni.co.uk>), Thomas Cook (website <www.thomascook.com>) and Airtours (website <www.airtours.com>).

GUIDES AND TOURS

There are numerous travel agencies in all the resorts and towns who can organise tours of the nearby sites. Check prices and quality before booking.

Licensed guides can be hired from the Egyptian Tourist Authority *(see page 125)* offices, or many large hotels can arrange the service for you. Only official guides are allowed to accompany tourists to archaeological sites. They can also be useful in helping you to get the best out of aspects of Cairo such as the old Islamic centre.

There is a well-organised network of tours from every town in Egypt and if you have not already pre-booked before your arrival you will be able to arrange these upon entering the country. Prices will be in US dollars and not all travel agents accept credit cards.

H

HEALTH AND MEDICAL CARE

While no inoculations are needed at present for your trip, do make inquiries with your doctor before travelling.

Malaria is only found in the El Fayyoum area – take precautions if you intend to visit the oasis and discuss the options with your doctor in good time before travelling.

Rabies is present in Egypt so take precautions to avoid being bitten by any animals.

Treat all scratches and cuts with antiseptic to avoid infection.

Do not drink the tap water – bottled water is safe and universally available.

Don't drink the Nile water, swim in it, or walk barefoot along its banks – the water contains bilharzias, a parasitic flatworm that is hazardous to human health.

The most common ailments relate to dehydration and upset stomachs. Take the following precautions to minimise the risks:

- Drink plenty of bottled water and always carry a supply with you when you are touring around.
- Go easy on alcohol as this will increase the effects of dehydration.
- Wash your hands before eating.
- Eat well-cooked meat and fruit without peel.
- Avoid ice in drinks except in luxury hotels.
- If you eat at buffets, make sure that any cold dishes have been kept well-chilled.
- Milk and dairy products may be unpasteurised in non-tourist establishments.

All large hotels have an English-speaking doctor on call should you become ill.

Pharmacies *(agzakhána)* have a green crescent sign decorated with a red cross or serpent. Local medicines may not have the same names as at home. Check with the hotel doctor before buying anything of which you are not sure.

All major towns have hospitals and most doctors speak a little English. The Anglo-American Hospital in Cairo is behind the Gazira Tower on Zamalek Island, tel: (2) 340 6162.

HITCHHIKING

Hitchhiking is not recommended and, given the new security measures for foreign travellers following the terrorist attacks in the 1990s, would be difficult, as all travel involving tourists is controlled in the central part of Egypt. Bus fares north of Cairo (towards Alexandria) are very reasonable. Travel from Luxor to Aswan, and from Luxor across to the Red Sea is controlled by the Egyptian military.

HOLIDAYS

The following days are secular holidays in Egypt.

1 January – banks only.

First Monday after Coptic Easter – National Spring Day.

25 April – Sinai Day.

1 May – Labour Day.

23 July – Revolution Day.

6 October – Armed Forces Day.

All Muslim holidays are celebrated in Egypt but shops are not necessarily closed. At Ramadan (dates change each year), when the Muslim population fasts during daylight hours, offices are open fewer hours, and shops close in the afternoon but remain open well into the night. Most restaurants stop selling alcohol (though not major hotels). Since the Islamic day starts at sunset most celebrations begin the night before the actual date.

L

LANGUAGE

Arabic is the official language of Egypt, and Egyptian Arabic is the 'standard' around the Arabic-speaking world, where there are hundreds of different regional 'dialects'.

Most people working in the tourist industry speak some English; in large hotels and tour agencies people speak good English. You will find local people, particularly children, practising a handful of English phrases on you.

Out in the deserts and oases you may find Egyptians who speak French rather than English as a second language.

LAUNDRY AND DRY CLEANING

Most hotels will be able to organise laundry and dry cleaning for you at extra cost for a same- or next-day service. This is probably the most sensible way to get your clothes laundered.

M

MAPS

The Egyptian Tourist Office issues basic maps for all the towns and some hotels distribute maps free of charge. Most towns are easy to explore but Cairo is relatively difficult. Hiring a guide is a good option; guides will be able to take you to all the major attractions and introduce you to some of the hidden districts of the capital.

MEDIA

TV: Egypt has three television channels. Channel II has daily news bulletins in English. All the major hotels have satellite TV allowing access to international news channels CNN and BBC News 24. Many also have other English-language entertainment channels.

Radio: There are two national radio stations; FM95 transmits news in English at 2.30pm and 8pm.

Newspapers: *The Egyptian Gazette* is published daily in English giving up-to-date news from around world, concentrating on Egypt and the Middle East. International newspapers are available at newsstands in major hotels, though some may be one day old.

MONEY

Currency: The currency of Egypt is the Egyptian pound, normally abbreviated to LE. This is divided into 100 piastres (pt). Bank notes are issued in the following denominations: 25pt, 50pt, 1LE, 5LE, 10LE, 20LE, 50LE and 100LE, coins in 5pt, 10pt, 20pt and 25pt.

Currency Exchange: Foreign currency must be exchanged with an official organisation; this may be a bank or official exchange office. Most large hotels have a small bank on the premises, which is open in the mornings and the evenings. The exchange rate is more favourable within Egypt so take minimal amounts with you into the country. Always obtain a receipt for your transaction as these may be checked on your exit from Egypt. Street banks are open from 8am–1pm Monday–Thursday.

Credit Cards: These are becoming more widely accepted in restaurants and shops. All major hotels will accept them in payment for rooms and services. You can use your credit card to obtain cash at banks with a small additional service charge. Take your passport and expect to wait for some time as security checks are made.

ATMs: ATMs are not widespread in Egypt. The major hotels in Cairo have machines in their lobbies, but do not rely on this as your only source of Egyptian currency.

Travellers' Cheques: These can be changed at banks and hotels but are not accepted for the purchase of goods.

O

OPEN HOURS

Banks are open Monday–Thursday 8am–1pm, though the smaller official bank offices in the large hotels are usually also open in the evenings to facilitate money changing.

In Cairo, shops are open 9am–7pm in winter and 9am–8pm in summer, closing one hour later on Monday and Thursday all year round.

Government shops are closed 2–5pm for a siesta and private shops may also close at hours to suit themselves.

Khan El Khalili bazaar is open until 8pm every day. In other tourist towns private shops open daily and stay open until late – often around 10pm.

During Ramadan, shops are often open longer hours – many stay open until after midnight, but they will always close for 30 minutes at sunset to take the fast-breaking *iftar* meal.

Government offices generally open Monday–Friday 9am–5pm, with a break from 11.30am–1.30pm on Friday. Airline offices remain open until 8pm.

Post Offices: Cairo's main post office is located at Ataba Square. It is open 24 hours a day except for Friday. Other post offices are open Saturday–Thursday 8.30am–3pm; Friday 8.30am–11.30am.

Museums and Archaeological Sites: Major museums are open daily from 8am and will stay open until 5pm – some sites such as Luxor, stay open until 10pm. Those with sound and light shows will restrict admittance in the evenings to a small number of ticketholders.

Smaller museums may be open in the mornings only. Most sites curtail opening hours during Ramadan.

P

POLICE

See *Crime and Safety for more details.*

Police 122
Cairo Tourist Police 126
The main police station in Cairo is at 5 Adly Street.

POST OFFICES

The postal service in Egypt is slow and unpredictable. If you want to send a package or something important or urgent it is better to send it by courier, and several of the major international companies have offices in the country.

Postboxes have no set colour or pattern, and you are probably better off using the facilities at your hotel – or any major hotel – to send your cards. These take at least 14 days to reach European destinations, and 18 days further afield.

Cairo's main post office is at Ataba Square. It is open 24 hours a day except on Friday. Other post offices open from 8.30am–3pm, except on Friday when it is 8.30am–11.30am.

PUBLIC TRANSPORT

Buses: A network of small buses operates services across Cairo but these are always over-crowded and often driven dangerously in addition to running along complicated routes. Several air-conditioned services a day link Cairo with Alexandria.
Metro: The Cairo metro links several parts of the city through Tahrir Square. Most useful for the visitor is the route to the Coptic museum and Old Cairo. Get off at Mar Girgis Station.
Boats: The Nile Bus operates a service along the river alongside Tahrir Square with the Coptic Museum and Old Cairo. The journey takes around 40 minutes. To get across the Nile at Luxor and Aswan use the traditional *felluca* sailboat, or the faster and cheaper diesel-engined ferries that work to a regular timetable.

There is also a car and passenger ferry from Hurghada to Sharm El Sheik that sails two days per week. Prices for foreigners are high.

Trains: There is a reliable fast service between Cairo and Alexandria. Services down the Nile are reliable, but enquire whether foreign travellers may use them, as they are not always guarded. An overnight luxury train operates to and from Luxor/Aswan; cabins must be pre-booked and prices are expensive; contact Wagons-lit, tel: (2) 349 2365.

Planes: Egypt Air (tel: 2 575 0600) operates a network of domestic services with Cairo at its hub; there are flights to Abu Simbel, Alexandria, Aswan, Hurghada, Luxor, Mersa Matru (on the Mediterranean coast), New Valley (in the Western Desert) and Sharm El-Sheikh.

It is wise to book ahead, confirm tickets and check in early (at least one hour before take-off), as overbooking is normal.

Horse-drawn carriages: The horse-drawn carriage, called a *calèche*, was the taxi of Egypt until recent times and you can still hire them for a stately ride in all the major Nile tourist towns: there are even some to be found in Cairo if you dare brave the roads in one. You can hire them for a journey back to your hotel, or a longer tour.

R

RELIGION

Egypt is a predominantly Muslim country with an 8 percent Coptic Christian minority and a tiny Jewish population.

Visitors should dress modestly, shake hands with the right hand and refrain from showing the sole of the foot when sitting on the ground. When you are visiting mosques, always remove your shoes.

Romantic physical contact between couples in public is not part of Egyptian social custom and is best avoided by visitors.

Muslims fast during the month of Ramadan, refraining from eating food during the hours of daylight. Many restaurants stay closed during the daytime and may serve special dishes rather than a full menu. Only tourist hotels and a few restaurants will serve alcohol at this time.

T

TELEPHONE

Egypt's telephone system is in the process of being upgraded and codes and numbers do change regularly; if you need to find out a current number or if the number you dial is no longer in use, call the operator on 140 and they will be able to help you; some operators speak English.

Most "Nilephone" public telephones in Aswan, Hurghada, Luxor, Sharm El-Sheikh accept cards for both international and domestic calls rather than coins. Phone cards are issued in units of 5, 10, 20 and 40. For international calls you will need one of 20 or 40 units.

Post offices have phone booths where you can make international calls and pay after you have finished your call.

Most large hotels have direct-dial international lines. These add a huge surcharge to the cost of your call but may be worth using as connections are sometimes more reliable. You can avoid the steep charges by using your credit card and direct-call centre, or a pre-pay international card with an international access number

The international code for Egypt is 20.

The internal area codes are:

Cairo 2
Aswan 97
Alexandria 3
Hurghada and the Red Sea coast 65
Luxor 95
The Sinai Peninsula 62

Egypt

International country codes are as follows, all prefixed by 00 when you make a call:

Australia 61
South Africa 27
Canada 1
United Kingdom 44
Ireland 353
United States 1
New Zealand 64

TIME ZONES

Egypt operates on GMT +2 hours. Clocks are put forward one hour in the summer.

TIPPING

In Egypt, the practice of tipping, or *backsheesh*, is widespread. You will probably come across local people (especially children) who approach you in the street asking for *backsheesh*. Although you don't need to give money to those who ask for it in this way, it is a good idea to carry plenty of small banknotes with you around town to give to those who provide a service, or who allow you into areas of temples that are not normally open to the public.

Another practice which is becoming popular in Egypt is for shopkeepers to agree to a lower price in exchange for tips.

The following people will expect tips for their services.

Bell boy	1LE per bag.
Maid	15LE per week.
Toilet attendant	1LE.
Waiter	10 percent unless service is included in the bill, in which case give small change.
Table boy	small change.

Tour Guide	10 percent.
Taxi driver	1–5LE
Felucca boatman	1LE per passenger.
Cruise Guide	40LE per client.

TOILETS

Good toilet facilities are generally found in museums and at all large hotels. Restaurants have toilets, although hygiene standards vary and you should buy a drink if you want to use the facilities.

TOURIST INFORMATION

The Egyptian Tourist Authority (ETA) is an excellent resource . For information before you travel, contact:

ETA
Misr Travel Tower
Abbassia Square, Cairo.
Tel: (2) 285 4509
Fax: (2) 285 4363
website <www.egypttourism.org>

USA
Egyptian State Tourist Office
630 Fifth Avenue, Suite 1706
New York, NY 10111.
Tel: (212) 332 2570
Fax: (212) 956 6439

USA
Egyptian State Tourist Office
645 North Michigan Avenue,
Suite 829
Chicago, IL 60611
Tel: (312) 280 4666
Fax: (312) 280 4788

Egyptian State Tourist Office
8383 Wilshire Boulevard,
Suite 215
Beverly Hills, CA 90211
Tel: (213) 653 8815
Fax: (213) 653 8961

UK
Egyptian State Tourist Office.
170 Piccadilly
London W1V 7DD
Tel: (020) 7493 5283
Fax: (020) 7408 0295

Canada
Egyptian State Tourist Office
1253 McGill College Avenue
#250, Montreal, Québec
H3B 2Y5
Tel: (514) 861 4420
Fax: (514) 861 8071

Egypt

In Egypt, there is tourist information at the following addresses:

Cairo: 5 Adly Street, tel: (2) 391 5434. You'll also find smaller offices at the pyramids and at Cairo International Airport.

Alexandria: Saad Zaghoul Square, tel: (3) 807 985.

Luxor: Nile Street, tel: (95) 382 215.

Aswan: Tourist Souk, tel: (97) 323 297.

Hurghada: Bank Misr Street, tel: (65) 444 420.

W

WEBSITES

Many useful websites have been included where they are pertinent throughout this A–Z section. The following sites will give you general information about Egypt and will provide links to other sites, allowing you to plan your itinerary more thoroughly before you travel.

<www.egyptsearch.com>

<www.egypt.net>

Several sections, including a special site for children with stories and information about the country and the culture.

<www.alexandriatour.com>

<www.luxorguide.com>

<www.egypthotelsdb.com> A comprehensive list of hotels but do not rely on their price guides as these may be out of date.

WEIGHTS AND MEASURES

Egypt operates on the metric system for weights and measures.

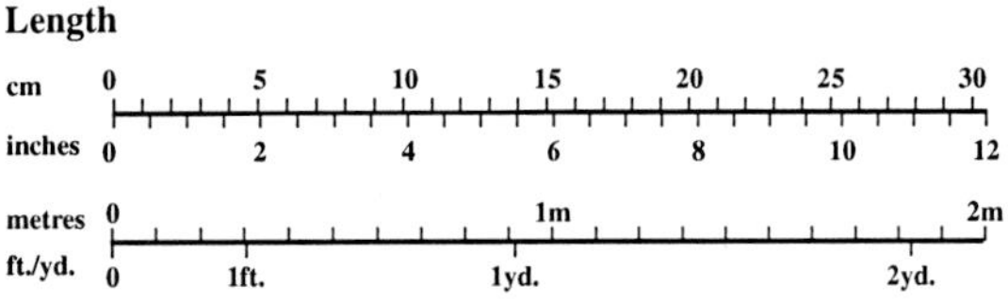

Weight

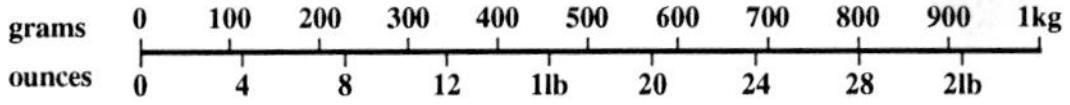

Fluid measures

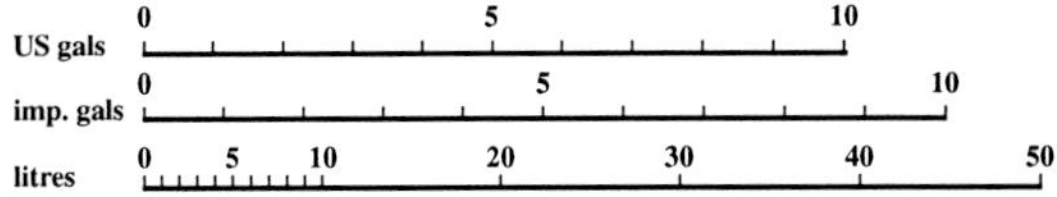

Distance

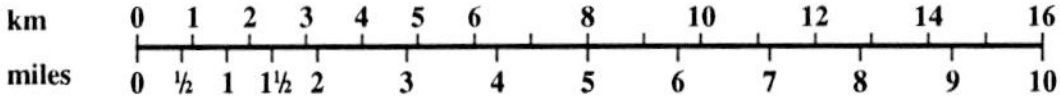

Temperature

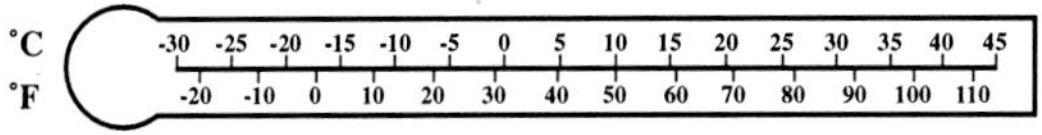

Y

YOUTH HOSTELS

There are youth hostels in Cairo and Alexandria, but the quality of accommodation varies and hostels are often fully booked well in advance. Pre-booking is always the best option. Contact the official International Youth Hotel Association in your own country or see <www.yha.org> for further information and advice.

Recommended Hotels

Egypt has numerous hotels; however, it is difficult to find good hotels in the lower price brackets so you should plan your budgets accordingly. Egyptian nationals and foreign residents will be offered cheaper prices than foreign visitors who will usually be asked to pay in US dollars – for this reason we have used US dollars for our own price guide. Rates are high if you don't pre-book, especially in the better-class hotels. It will save you money if you book your accommodation through a travel agent before you travel.

The following recommendations cover hotels in all the major tourist towns with a range of options from budget to expensive. We have also added a recommendation for a Nile cruise. Some hotels have scant address information. Rest assured that your correspondence will arrive there, but for speed we suggest faxing or e-mailing questions or reservation requests.

Service charges of 12 percent are added to bills at larger up-scale hotels. Municipal tax of 2 percent and a sales tax of 5 percent will always be added to the bill.

To contact hotels from outside Egypt dial 20 and the regional code in brackets.

$ below $40
$$ $40–$80
$$$ $80–$120
$$$$ $120–$160
$$$$$ above $160

CAIRO

The Mena House Oberoi Hotel and Casino $$$$$ *Pyramids Road, Giza, tel: (2) 383 3222; fax: (2) 383 7777; website*

<www.oberoihotels.com>. Historic Cairo mansion built for the opening of the Suez Canal (when it housed VIPs visiting the pyramids), which sits just metres away from its entrance. Now a Grand Dame of Cairo hotels – the lines of the historic wing have a certain timeless elegance, and there are newer rooms built around the expansive swimming pool. Rooms have A/C, satellite TV, mini-bar, hairdryer and safe. Facilities include two restaurants, a bar, pool, casino and golf course. 523 rooms. Major credit cards.

Cairo Marriott $$$$–$$$$$ *Sayara El Gezira Street, P.O. Box 33 Zamalek, Cairo, tel: (2) 340 8888; fax: (2) 340 6667; website <www.marriott.com>*. The heart of the Cairo Marriott is the old riverside royal residence of Khedive Ismael, built in 1869 to coincide with the opening of the Suez Canal. This period building is now occupied by a reception and the casino. Two high-rise modern towers house most of the rooms. Rooms have A/C, satellite TV, hairdryer, mini-bar, bathrobes and complimentary newspaper. Facilities include pool, health club, tennis courts, casino, 11 eateries, entertainment, 24-hour room service, shopping arcade and hair salon. 1250 Rooms. Major credit cards.

Le Meridien Pyramids $$$$$ *El Ramaya Square, Giza, P.O. Box 25 Pyramids, Cairo, tel: (2) 383 0383; fax: (2) 383 1730; website <www.meridien_pyramids.com.eg>*. Situated within strolling distance of the pyramids, this elegant modern hotel offers every comfort with a range of dining opportunities. Rooms have A/C, satellite TV, phone, mini-bar, hairdryer. Non-smoking rooms available. Facilities include five restaurants, five bars, 24-hour room service, shopping arcade, gym, tennis courts and a spa. Wheelchair access. 523 rooms. Major credit cards.

The Cosmopolitan Hotel $$ *1 Ibn Taalab Street, Cairo; tel: (2) 393 3956; fax: (2) 393 3531*. This Art Deco hotel is situated downtown in the recently rejuvenated area of the old Bourse. The hotel has also been renovated without losing any of its belle époque character. All the architectural detail remains with the simple rooms furnished in period style furniture. An interesting option for budget travellers with more charm than many street hotels. Rooms have TV and phone. Facilities include restaurant, café, bar and business centre. 84 rooms. Major credit cards.

The Carlton Hotel $-$$ *21, July 26th Street, Ezbekiya, Cairo, tel: (2) 575 5232; fax: (2) 575 5323.* A very modest but clean hotel in the heart of Cairo within easy reach of the main attractions. Simple decorations and furnishings. 60 rooms. Major credit cards.

ALEXANDRIA AND THE MEDITERRANEAN

El Salamlek Palace Hotel $$$$$ *Montazah Gardens, Alexandria, tel: (3) 547 7999; fax: (3) 547 3585.* Built in 1892 as a hunting lodge, this was the palace of King Farouk before his abdication in 1952. An intimate hotel, which manages to make guests feel as if they are part of a house party, the El Salamlek Palace was recently totally refurbished, although it still retains many of its period features. Public areas are decorated with original art and fine antiques. Rooms have A/C, TV and phone. Facilities include a gourmet restaurant, private beach, casino, flower shop, hair salon and 24-hour room service. 20 rooms. Major credit cards.

Montazah Sheraton $$$$-$$$$$ *Corniche Road Montazah, Alexandria, tel: (3) 548 0550; fax: (3) 540 1331.* A giant modern hotel that is situated across from King Farouk's old palace. Rooms have A/C, satellite TV, phone, hairdryer and balcony. Facilities include five restaurants, pool, bars, tennis courts, shops, hair and beauty salon, and 24-hour room service. 279 rooms. Major credit cards.

The Paradise Inn-Metropole Hotel $$$ *52 Saad Zaghoul Street, Alexandria, tel: (3) 482 1465; fax: (3) 428 2040.* A beautiful early 20th century hotel decorated throughout in Louis XIV style – the huge heavy doors, wallpapered ceilings and heavy drapes of the ornate communal areas could have come from a French chateau. Situated on the main square in the city, it is ideally located for touring. Rooms are of differering sizes and are all well-furnished; those at the rear have sea views. Rooms have A/C, TV and phone. Facilities include a good Egyptian restaurant. 30 rooms. Major credit cards.

THE NILE VALLEY

The Old Cataract Hotel $$$$ *Abtal El Tahrir Street, Aswan, tel: (97) 316 000; fax: (97) 316 01.* Harking back to the days of elegant Edwardian Grand Tours, the Old Cataract Hotel has become a landmark in Aswan and has seen such illustrious guests as Winston Churchill and Agatha Christie, who wrote *Death on the Nile* while staying here. The Nile looks wonderful from the hotel's elegant terrace and gardens. Interior décor is period. Ask for a room with river view. Rooms have A/C, satellite TV, phone and tea and coffee. Facilities include an excellent restaurant, pool, bar and parking. Buffet breakfast is compulsory and charged to your bill (currently 46.50LE). 131 rooms. Major credit cards.

Sofitel Winter Palace Hotel $$$-$$$$ *Khalid Ibn El Waleed Street, Luxor, tel: (95) 380 923; fax: (95) 380 972.* The Grand Dame of Luxor hotels, built on the banks of the Nile in 1886, the Winter Palace still makes a statement with its façade of rosy-coloured stucco work. The interior spaces are expansive and rooms have lofty ceilings and French-style windows. Updated and modernised in 1994, it is still best enjoyed for its period charm. Ask for a room with a river view. Rooms have A/C, satellite TV, phone and mini-bar. Facilities include a large heated pool, tennis and squash courts, gardens, two restaurants, coffee shop, shops and entertainment. Free airport transfer. 136 rooms. Major credit cards.

Hotel Hathor $ *Nile Street, Aswan, tel: (97) 314 580; no fax.* A clean and friendly budget option on the corniche. The prices are incredibly cheap – well below the **$** limit – but this is definitely a no-frills place. It's popular with the young travelling crowd so people stay a couple of days and then move on. Its location right at the heart of town is hard to beat. Facilities include a pool on the roof. Breakfast included in the price. Cash only.

St. Joseph Hotel $ *Khaled Ebn El Walad Street, Luxor, tel: (95) 381 707; fax: (95) 381 727.* A good budget option, the St. Joseph is clean and nicely furnished. Situated a five-minute walk south of the corniche on the main street, it is surrounded by several larger, more expensive hotels and a range of Egyptian eateries. Rooms have A/C, phone, TV and balcony, and many have Nile views. Facilities include restaurant, bar, roof pool and shop. 75 rooms. Major credit cards.

RED SEA AND SINAI

Oberoi Sal Hasheesh $$$$$ *P.O. Box 117, Hurghada, Red Sea, tel: (65) 440 777; fax: (65) 440 778; website <www.oberoihotels.com>.* This suites-only resort is one of the newest and without a doubt the smartest on the Red Sea coast. The elegant décor has rich elements of traditional Islamic design and the rooms are beautifully appointed. Each suite has its own private courtyard, some including their very own swimming pool. Expansive gardens and attentive service make the Sal Hasheesh the ideal place to recharge your spiritual and physical batteries. Suites have living room, A/C, satellite TV, phone and computer-point, safe and mini-bar with tea/coffee. Facilities include private beach, pool, gourmet restaurant, bar, library, massage rooms and sauna. 104 suites. Major credit cards.

Ritz Carlton $$$$$ *Om El Seed, P.O. Box 72, Sharm El Skeikh, Sinai, tel: (62) 661 917; fax: (62) 661 785; website <www.ritzcarlton.com>.* The place to come for a luxury stay on the Sinai. The hotel is intimate and elegantly designed with large, beautifully decorated rooms. Personal and attentive service is guaranteed and just about everything you want can be organised by the concierge. Rooms have A/C, satellite TV, phone, safe and hairdryer – non-smoking rooms are available. Facilities include spa, 18-hole golf course, pool, six restaurants, two bars, fitness centre, tennis courts, kid's club, 24-hour room service, shuttle bus and complimentary shoeshine. 30 rooms. Major credit cards.

Hilton Taba Resort $$$$$ *Taba Beach, Sinai, tel: (69) 430 140; fax: (69) 578 044.* Large resort overlooking the Israeli border. Rooms have A/C, TV, phone, mini-bar and hairdryer. Facilities include restaurants, bars, pool, shops and room service. 410 rooms. Major credit cards.

Morganland $$$ *St. Catherine's, Sinai, tel: (62) 470 404; fax: (62) 470 331; (reservations and information in Cairo, tel: (2) 796 2437; fax: (2) 796 4104).* Situated in a spectacular location amongst the mountains of the Sinai, Morganland is a five-minute drive from St. Catherine's Monastery. Rooms are very spacious though simply furnished and set around a spectacular swimming pool. Each room has a balcony or a terrace to make the most of the fabulous views. Rooms have A/C, TV and phone. Facilities include a rustic restaurant and a Bedouin bazaar. 220 rooms. Major credit cards.

Sunlight Rosetta Hotel $$$ *Na'am Bay, Sharm El Sheikh, Sinai, tel: (62) 601 888; fax: (62) 601 999.* Expansive holiday complex rising up a slight hill just across the street from Na'am Bay's main beach and only minutes on foot to its numerous eateries and nightlife. There's a bright and airy feel and clusters of low-rise blocks sit around the three pools. Good for couples and families, the hotel is located next door to the busiest and arguably the best dive shop in town. Rooms have A/C, satellite

TV, phone and fridge. Facilities include three pools, three restaurants and a bar. 102 rooms. Major credit cards.

Le Pacha Resort $$ *Corniche Road, Hurghada, Red Sea, tel: (65) 444 150; fax: (65) 443 705.* One of the oldest hotels in Hurghada, the La Pacha certainly looks a little careworn and dated, but it has good facilities and is a passable option for those who don't want to pay 5-star prices. It's on the beach but in the midst of all the action at night. Rooms have TV, mini-bar and balcony/terrace. Facilities include restaurant, bar, pool. 169 rooms. Major credit cards.

Zak Royal Wings Hotel $ *Corniche Road, Hurghada, Red Sea, tel: (65) 446 012; fax: (65) 446 013.* Clean and basic rooms in this hotel just off the main street. Rooms have A/C, TV, phone, fridge and balcony or terrace. Facilities include large swimming pool, restaurant and on-site bar. Dinner and bed-and-breakfast rates available. 41 rooms. Major credit cards.

NILE CRUISE

Oberoi Nile Cruises $$$$$ *Regional sales office, Mena House Oberoi, Pyramids Road, Giza, Cairo, tel: (2) 383 3222; fax: (2) 383 3444; website <www.oberoihotels.com>.* The Oberoi group operates four Nile cruises offering 3–6 day itineraries. All the vessels are luxurious but there are differences between them. Shehrayar and Shehrazad have 31 spacious cabins (the largest currently on the Nile) with two bathrooms per cabin. They accommodate a maximum of 70 guests on any trip. They also have their own berths at Aswan and Luxor – no tramping through several other boats to get to the shore. Philae has large French windows in all its 58 cabins. It also has a small gym. All vessels offer excellent service, all meals are included, and there are fully guided tours. Cabins have A/C, satellite TV, mini-bar and safe. Facilities include restaurant, bar, shop and pool. Major credit cards.

Recommended Restaurants

Egypt has developed a wide range of good international restaurants, often linked to large hotels, where you can enjoy food prepared and served to a high standard. These are more expensive than local restaurants but no more than you would pay for an equivalent meal at home, and maybe a little less. All hotels welcome non-residents at their restaurants.

The following recommendations cover all the major tourist towns in Egypt and include Egyptian and international restaurants in all price ranges. We have included elegant period dining rooms and beach eateries, casual and formal, to give you the choice to suit your mood. Although we have given a price indication in Egyptian pounds, you may find menus priced in US Dollars and may even be charged in US Dollars. Where reservations are recommended it is indicated in the description.

If you are making a reservation from within the town or city, do not dial the regional code. To contact hotels from outside Egypt dial 20 and the regional code in brackets.

$ under 40LE

$$ 40LE–70LE

$$$ 70LE–100LE

$$$$ 100LE–140LE

$$$$$ over 140LE

CAIRO

The Moghul Room $$$$$ *Oberoi Mena House Hotel, Pyramids Road Giza, tel: (2) 383 3222.* The best Indian cuisine in the city, perhaps one of the best outside India – not surprisingly given the Oberoi's Indian antecedents – the Moghul room offers excellent cuisine, attentive service and intimate ambience. Live Indian music accompanies the meal. Open daily noon–3pm, 7.30pm–12.30am. Reservations recommended. Major credit cards.

Le Champollion $$$$$ *Le Meridien Cairo Hotel, Corniche El-Nil, Garden City, tel: (2) 362 1717.* One of the newest restaurants in town, Le Champollion has already become a favourite place for that special meal. The river-level restaurant offers wonderful views and the Mediterranean cuisine is exquisite. A good option for a more formal evening. Open daily 7pm–midnight. Reservations recommended. Major credit cards.

The Grill $$$$$ *Seramis Inter-Continental Hotel, Corniche El-Nil, Garden City, tel: (2) 795 7171.* One of the best restaurants in the city, The Grill is frequented by businessmen negotiating deals, couples having a romantic meal, and discerning vistors who come for the elegant formal service and wonderful food, not to mention the Nile view. International cuisine. Open daily 7pm–midnight. Reservations recommended. Major credit cards.

Khan El Khalili Restaurant $$$–$$$$$ *5 El Baddistan Lane, Khan El Khalili, Cairo, tel: (2) 590 3788.* An excellent Egyptian restaurant in the heart of Khan El Khalili bazaar. The restaurant has atmospheric Islamic décor and good food – this is a great place to get into authentic Egyptian cuisine and you'll certainly feel as though you've arrived in a totally different culture, and the service is reassuringly stylish. The kitchens are overseen by an international hotel group. Open daily 11am–11pm. Major credit cards.

Roy's Country Kitchen $$$ *Cairo Marriott Sayara El Gezira Street, P.O. Box 33 Zamalek, Cairo, tel: (2) 340 8888 ext. 8493; website <www.marriott.com>.* All-American diner with an expansive range of à la carte and buffet options. If you like waffles, chicken wings, hamburgers or gumbo, then this is the place to come. Service is relaxed and dishes are cooked to order. Open daily 24 hours. Major credit cards.

La Pacha 1901 $$–$$$$ *Saray El Gezirak Street, Zamalek, tel: (2) 735 6730; website <www.lepacha.com>*. This floating palace on the Nile was built in 1901. It has been thoroughly refurbished and extended to offer a range of eleven restaurants and bars. There's an English pub, a French bistro and an Italian trattoria, as well as a traditional Egyptian eatery. Open daily 6pm–11pm. Major credit cards.

Laredo Steak House $$–$$$ *Le Meridien Pyramids Hotel, El Ramaya Square, Giza, P.O. Box 25 Pyramids, Cairo, tel: (2) 383 0383; website <www.meridien_pyramids.com.eg>*. Diners have to walk through the swinging doors to this Western steak house. Wooden ranch-style furniture sets the scene and the menu includes grilled meats, spare ribs, chilli, Mexican dishes and a range of sandwiches. There are a range of international beers. Open daily 5pm–midnight. Major credit cards.

Alfi Bay Restaurant $$ *3 El-Alfi Street, Downtown, tel: (2) 577 1888.* Established in 1936, this restaurant serves excellent Egyptian food, specialising in *kofta* and stuffed pigeon. A loyal local clientele means there is a genuine Egyptian atmosphere. Open daily 6pm–11pm. Cash only.

Andrea $ *59–60 Marioutiya Canal, Giza, tel: (2) 383 1133.* Extremely good Egyptian restaurant serving a range of local cuisine, including grilled meats and salads. In summer you can eat in the airy gardens, and there is a dining room for the chillier winter evenings. Lunchtime is always busy with tour groups. For a more authentic atmosphere try to visit in the evenings. The portions are large so bring a hearty appetite. Open daily noon–midnight. Cash only.

El-Fishawi Coffee Shop $ *Fishawi Street, Khan El Khalili, Cairo; no phone.* At this long-established coffee and smoking shop, you can stop for a drink and watch Cairenes go about their daily business. This is the place where locals come to read the newspapers, play backgammon or smoke a hookah. It's a good place to try one if it strikes your fancy, and you'll be given lots of advice to help you get the most out of your special smoking experience. Open daily 8am–11pm. Cash only.

ALEXANDRIA AND THE MEDITERRANEAN

Al-Farouk Restaurant $$$$$ *at the El Salamlek Palace Hotel, Montazah Gardens, Alexandria, tel: (3) 547 7999.* The impressive period dining room, replete with marble columns and wood panelling, is fit for the king who used to live here before his abdication. High French cuisine is served in formal style; the Al-Farouk is the place to go for a special occasion. Open daily noon–4pm, 8pm–1am. Reservations recommended. Major credit cards.

Santa Lucia $$ *40 Safia Zaghoul Street, Alexandria, tel: (3) 482 0371.* A long-established restaurant with local and Italian dishes, the Santa Lucia is situated in the heart of town. Regular live music makes it popular with locals and visitors. Open daily 6pm–11pm. Major credit cards.

Taverna El Ramel $–$$ *Saad Zaghoul Square, Alexandria, tel: (3) 482 8189.* You'll find this cheerful café-style eatery at the tram terminal in the heart of town. Staff serve a range of Greek dishes as well as Egyptian food, and you can get meals to take out. A good place to watch the world go by. Open daily 11am–11pm. Cash only.

Trianon $ *56 Midan Sa'ad Zaghoul, Alexandria; no phone.* An authentic Art Deco tea room harking back to the days of

European rule. There are teas, ice creams and light snacks; a visit is thoroughly recommended just to take in the bustling Alexandria atmosphere. Open daily 9am–11pm. Cash only.

THE NILE VALLEY

La Perla $$$$$ *The Oberoi Hotel, Elephanitine Island, P.O. Box 62, Aswan, tel: (97) 314 666.* Set across the river from the main part of town, you can take a romantic sail across to the Oberoi to La Perla. Modern décor with the accent on Italian food. Open daily noon–3pm, 7pm–11pm. Major credit cards.

The 1886 $$$$$ *Sofitel Winter Palace Hotel, Khalid Ibn El Waleed Street, Luxor, tel: (95) 380 923.* This gourmet restaurant features Egyptian and Continental European dishes. Set in a fine period dining room, it's easy to imagine the grand soirées of yesteryear. Silver service – so somewhere to visit on special occasions. Open daily 6pm–10.30pm. Major credit cards.

The 1902 $$$$$ *The Old Cataract Hotel, Abtal El Tahrir Street, Aswan, tel: (97) 316 000.* The grand Moorish-style dining room frequented by Winston Churchill and Agatha Christie is one reason to eat at this restaurant; the atmosphere takes you back to the days of the Grand Tour with muffled conversation and clinking glasses. Formal dining, though it is a shame there isn't a terrace. The food is mainly Southern European and Egyptian. Open daily noon–3pm, 7pm–midnight. Reservations recommended. Major credit cards.

Lotus $$$–$$$$ *Novotel, Khaled Ibn El Waleed Street, Luxor, tel: (95) 380 925.* This large floating restaurant offers all day service while tethered at the Nile's bank (there's a sun deck and whirlpool to enjoy). There's also an evening cruise with dinner included. Regional and international dishes. Open daily 9am–6pm, dinner 7pm. Reservations are recommended for dinner. Major credit cards.

Aswan Moon $–$$ *Corniche El-Nil, Aswan; no phone.* This floating restaurant on the Nile is one of the best of the local restaurants in town. There's nothing fancy on the menu but the grilled chicken, kebabs and *kofta* are well-cooked, though the recently introduced pizzas will be a disappointment to aficionados. Service is friendly and efficient and they also sell alcohol, which their neighbours don't. Open daily 11am–11pm. Major credit cards.

Jamboree Restaurant $–$$ *Mumtazah Street (near the Brooke Hospital for Sick Animals), Luxor; no phone.* This British-owned café/restaurant is sparkling clean with stiff table linen and freshly cut flowers. You can find Egyptian dishes on the menu but most clients seem to prefer the English/Indian fusion and Italian options. Open daily 10.30am–2.30pm, 6.30pm–11pm. Cash only.

Chez Omar $ *Youssef Hassan Square (in the middle of the bazaar), Luxor; no phone.* This tiny green oasis sits amid the bustle of the market and is a great place to rest your feet after a hard day's shopping. The menu is basic but pleasing – grilled meats, chicken, fish, plus Egyptian desserts – and it's cooked in the kitchens of the Venus Hotel across the street. Open daily 8am–11pm. Cash only.

THE RED SEA AND THE SINAI

Blue Ginger $$$$$ *Ritz Carlton Hotel, Om El Seed, P.O. Box 72, Sharm El Skeikh, Sinai, tel: (62) 661 919.* Master chef Raymond Koh reigns over a kitchen producing an amazing array of Asian delicacies, including Japanese, Thai, Malaysian, Chinese, Singaporean and Korean. The flavours are authentic and the ingredients very fresh. Keeping to the exotic Oriental theme, there are black marble-lined pools and strings of colourful Chinese lanterns. Sake and Chinese wines are available. Open daily 6.30pm– 10.30pm. Major credit cards.

Il Foro Restaurant $$–$$$ *Sheraton Road, Hurghada, tel: (65) 442 247.* A very pretty European-style dining room with elegant cutlery and glassware sets the scene in Il Foro. The menu is Italian, with pasta, pizza and meat dishes along with a good choice of fresh local fish. Open kitchen. Open daily 6pm–11pm. Major credit cards.

Moby Dick $$–$$$ *Sheraton Road, Hurghada (opposite the Helnan Regina Hotel), tel: (65) 440 050.* As the name suggests, lots of seafood on the menu here along with grilled chicken and meat dishes. Snacks also available. Lively patio for evening dining. Open daily 6pm–11pm. Cash only.

Hard Rock Café $–$$$ *Marina Street, Na'am Bay Sharm El Sheik, tel: (2) 738 0492.* Burgers, sandwiches and salads from the ubiquitous café chain. Open daily 1pm–1am. Major credit cards.

Baby Fish Restaurant $–$$ *On the seafront, Dahab; no phone.* Right on the beach at Dahab you couldn't find a better place for a relaxed lunch – you don't even need shoes or a shirt. Fresh fish and grilled meats are the basis of the simple menu and you can enjoy the view because the service is relaxed. Open daily noon–11pm. Cash only.

El Dawr $–$$ *Restaurant Na'am Bay at the Rosetta Hotel, tel: (62) 601888.* Excellent Egyptian cuisine served in the open-air restaurant – traditionally designed to mimic a Bedouin tent with long seats decorated with cushions and covered with a high tent. Food is cooked to order at the open grill so you can see exactly what's happening. A good introduction to local cuisine. Open daily 6pm–10.30pm. Major credit cards.

INDEX